THE
EVERYDAY
LIGHT-HEARTED
COOKBOOK

THE
EVERYDAY
LIGHT-HEARTED
COOKBOOK

ANNE LINDSAY

GRUB STREET · LONDON

Published by Grub Street, The Basement, 10 Chivalry Road, London SW11 1HT

First UK impression 1994 (Reprinted 1995)

ACKNOWLEDGEMENTS

The Heart and Stroke Foundation of Canada would like to thank the following people for reviewing the introductory chapter. Their expertise helped present Canada's Guidelines for Healthy Eating in a meaningful way. Leslie Berndl, M.Sc, R.P.Dt; Carmen Connolly M.A., R.P.Dt; Carol Dombrow B.Sc, R.P.Dt; Barbara Engle R.P.Dt; Susan Fyshe, M.H.Sc, R.P.Dt; Lynn Garrison, M.H.Sc, R.P.Dt; Anthony Graham, M.D, F.R.C.P.(C); Jean Harvey M.H.Sc, R.P.Dt; Julie Lacasse M.Sc, R.P.Dt; Richard Lauzon, PhD, M.B.A; Bretta Maloff, B.H.Ec, M.Ed, R.D; Margaret Metzger, R.P.Dt; Gerald Wong, M.D, F.R.C.P.C.

The Library Cataloguing in Publication Data
Lindsay, Anne
    Everyday Light-Hearted Cooking
    I. Title
    641.5

    ISBN 0-948817-78-X

Illustrations by Madeleine David
Photography by Clive Webster
Food styling by Olga Truchan
Cover photo: Harvest Vegetable Curry
Typesetting by BMD Graphics, Hemel Hempstead
Printed and bound by Biddles Ltd, Guildford and King's Lynn

Contents

AUTHOR'S ACKNOWLEDGEMENTS

Anyone who hasn't been part of writing a healthy eating cookbook could never imagine the large number of people involved. I have the enjoyable task of cooking and writing but that is just a small part in the total work involved to produce this book. A few behind-the-scenes workers whom I would like to thank are:

Shannon Graham, my friend, dietician and co-worker who has helped with recipe testing for all my cookbooks.
Nancy Williams, my sister-in-law, who researches and keeps my office in order.
Carol Dombrow, nutritionist, Heart and Stroke Foundation of Canada, who has put many hours into reading the manuscript and co-ordinating the nutritional analysis.
Denise Beatty, for writing such a wonderful introduction and always being available to consult.
Elizabeth Baird, friend and food editor at *Canadian Living* magazine for her help and support.

Many, many thanks to my family, first to my husband, Bob, for his constant support and excellent advice, and for doing the family grocery shopping on Saturday mornings when I worked. Thanks to my daughter, Susie, sons Jeff and John, my most honest critics and usually willing dishwashers for all the great dinners we have together.

I would like to thank the British Heart Foundation for their support of this book, and Anne Heughan for editing.

Many thanks to Grub Street for their enthusiasm for my cookbook.

To everyone who has bought this book, I hope it will help you have delicious dinners and mealtimes you enjoy every day. Your appreciation and regular use of my cookbooks makes me very happy.

Preface

There is a widespread suspicion that healthy living means
sacrificing all that is enjoyable in life, particularly when it
comes to food. Not so! Food is one of the great joys of life and
the recipes contained within *The Everyday Light-Hearted
Cookbook* are proof of that.

Coronary disease remains the single most frequent cause
of premature death in the United Kingdom and dietary
factors play a significant part in its development.
Unfortunately, a great deal of misleading information has
been written which this volume helps to correct.
Some writers take great delight in emphasizing apparent
inconsistencies in dietary advice but it is inevitable that as
our understanding of heart disease and its origins grows, so
advice may change in detail although the overall message
remains consistent. Debate over the relative merits of
polyunsaturates and monounsaturates is far less important
than the generally acknowledged need for adults to reduce
their overall consumption of fat. Healthy eating is not based
on a long list of don'ts resulting in a dull and uninteresting
diet but instead leads to the discovery of a whole range of
new tastes and delights that we have either forgotten or never
experienced.

A healthy diet is of course only part of the campaign
against heart disease, albeit an important part. Quitting
cigarettes is an essential feature of any plan to reduce the toll
of coronary disease; fortunately cigarette smoking is
declining in the United Kingdom but even here there are
worrying signs like the increase in smoking among young
girls. Regular physical activity is also of value, not only in the
prevention of heart disease but in a whole variety of ways
that lead to good health including a contribution to the
prevention of osteoporosis. Physical activity should be
regular and "aerobic" like walking, swimming, dancing and
jogging; it does not need to be either exhausting,
competitive or very skillful! Many people would find
physical activity more enjoyable and continue it into adult

life if it was not associated with athletic prowess and competition. All of us can find a form of physical recreation that is enjoyable without the need to be a "winner"; exercising the dog or walking round the park or city centre at lunchtime is of potential value as regular exercise.

The overriding message of this book and indeed of the British Heart Foundation's campaign for the prevention of heart disease is that to get healthy and stay healthy involves no tedious self denial but a far more enjoyable and fulfilling life-style than before.

Bon appetit!

Professor B L Pentecost MD FRCP
Medical Director
British Heart Foundation

INTRODUCTION TO A HEALTHIER LIFESTYLE

If you're interested in healthy eating, chances are you're no stranger to Anne Lindsay's cookbook for healthy heart cooking, *The Light-Hearted Cookbook*. Spurred on by its bestseller success and the tremendous demand for healthier recipes, Anne has created more great-tasting recipes in this sequel, *The Everyday Light-Hearted Cookbook*.

As in *The Light-Hearted Cookbook*, these new recipes are both healthy and delicious. Although there are some special occasion recipes, this cookbook is geared more to family-style cooking and everyday meals. The recipes can be made simply and quickly – a must for busy, active families.

The book starts with the most up-to-date information on what healthy eating is all about and you'll find suggestions for making healthy eating a part of your everyday life. There's also information on how to plan healthy meals, shop for healthy food, and choose wisely when eating out.

And then, to bring healthy eating into your kitchen and onto your table, there are more than 200 fabulous family-style recipes waiting to be tried. From appetizers to desserts, you'll discover that eating can be both healthy and enjoyable.

GUIDELINES FOR HEALTHY EATING

Advice on healthy eating has been provided by the government and health authorities for many years. From time to time it's necessary to take a fresh look at the advice and update it, based on the latest nutrition research. This task was just recently undertaken by The Department of Health and in 1991 The Health Education Authority produced *Enjoy Healthy Eating*[1]. *The Everyday Light-Hearted Cookbook* is based on these new dietary recommendations. Their purpose is to promote and maintain health among people over the age of two while reducing the risk of nutrition-related diseases.

The way to healthy eating

— Enjoy your food.

— Eat a variety of foods.

— Eat plenty of foods rich in starch or complex carbohydrate and fibre.

— Don't eat too much fat.

— Don't eat sugary foods too often.

— Look after the vitamins and minerals in your food.

— If you drink, keep within sensible limits.

— Eat the right amount to be a healthy weight.

---

[1] Source: Dietary Reference Values for Food Energy and Nutrients for the United Kingdom, Department of Health 1991.

HEALTHY EATING MADE EASY

In the last ten years, our understanding of how diet affects health has come a long way. However, the reporting of this information often fails to put the newer discoveries into perspective. As a result, some people are more confused than ever, believing that good nutrition and healthy eating is more complex than it really is.

Healthy eating is eating to promote good health. While healthy eating can't guarantee that you'll never suffer from heart disease, cancer, diabetes or excess body weight, it can help to stack the odds in your favour. Healthy eating can help reduce the risk of these nutrition-related diseases while it promotes and maintains health in general.

Below, each guideline is discussed in more detail, and will show you how to put these ideas into action.

ENJOY A VARIETY OF FOODS

The very basis of healthy eating is balance: a balance between getting enough of the essential nutrients without getting too much of any one nutrient, particularly one like fat.

It stands to reason that it's going to be more difficult to have a healthy diet if you eat only a limited number of foods, particularly if these foods are high in fat and low in fibre. But if you eat as many different foods as possible, you're more likely to get all the nutrients you need and less likely to be always eating poor-quality foods.

Eating a varied diet means that you're always changing foods, trying new ones, maybe experimenting with different ethnic foods. And as you'll soon find out it also means trying new ways of preparing foods.

However, to give some practical meaning to this guideline, consider these signs of a varied diet:

— eat eight or ten different vegetables over the course of a couple of weeks instead of alternating beween peas and carrots;

— keep more than apples and bananas in your fruit bowl;

— plan your dinner menus using various protein foods such as fish, beans, pulses, beef, pork and lamb instead of eating chicken five nights a week;

— eat different kinds of foods rich in complex carbohydrates including bread, pasta, rice, breakfast cereals, plantains, potatoes;

— vary your packed lunches each day; you might use different breads to make sandwiches; other days you might have pasta salad instead of a sandwich; sometimes pack milk instead of fruit juice; some days include canned fruit, other days use fresh fruit;

— sometimes drink milk, other times choose cheese or yogurt.

EAT PLENTY OF FOODS RICH IN STARCH OR COMPLEX CARBOHYDRATES AND FIBRE

This guideline aims to increase your consumption of the complex carbohydrates or starchy foods, and of dietary fibre. Healthy eaters will want to plan more of their meals around these foods because they are:

— very nutritious;

— low in dietary fat and calories;

— the key sources of dietary fibre.

By basing your meals primarily on these foods and using animal-protein foods such as meat, cheese and eggs as adjuncts to the meal, you will find it easier to keep your fat intake at a healthy level and get more than enough dietary fibre.

Beans and pulses are fabulous sources of complex carbohydrates and soluble dietary fibre. They comprise all the dried peas and beans including such things as lentils, butter beans, black-eyed beans, soybeans, chick-peas, kidney beans, pinto beans, black or white beans, and split peas. Other than baked beans and split pea soup, people tend to shy away from other beans because they don't know what do with them. So make a point of trying the recipes that use all of these because they are delicious and they're a great way to have a low-fat, high-fibre meal.

Menus Rich in Complex Carbohydrates and Dietary Fibre

To put this guideline into use, put some of these meals on your plate.

Red Bean Salad with Feta and Red Pepper	page 65
Southwest Rice and Bean Salad	page 73
Bean and Vegetable Burritos	page 174
Chinese Rice and Vegetable Stir-Fry	page 182
Pasta e Fagioli	page 149
Linguine with Asparagus and Red Pepper	page 150

Where Fibre Fits In

Most of us do not get enough fibre each day. It's estimated that most people need approximately twice as much as they're getting now. That amounts to about 30 grams of fibre each day. It sounds like a lot of fibre, but it's not hard to get if you choose the right foods. Fibre comes in different forms and from different kinds of foods. Not surprisingly, the different fibres have different effects on you.

Soluble Dietary Fibre

Soluble fibre is a soft fibre that seems to help in the control of blood sugar and in the lowering of blood cholesterol, especially if it's unusually high. Oat products are one of the best-known sources of soluble fibre.

The Best Sources of Soluble Fibre

- oat bran

- oatmeal

- dried peas and beans, lentils

- pectin-rich fruits: apples, strawberries, citrus fruits

- barley

Insoluble Dietary Fibre

Wheat bran is the best-known insoluble dietary fibre. Once called roughage, this type of fibre helps to prevent and control bowel problems and may be important in the prevention of certain cancers.

The Best Sources of Insoluble Fibre

- wheat bran and wheat bran cereals

- whole grain foods like wholemeal bread

- fruits and vegetables, including skins and seeds when practical

---

Fibre Tips for Everyday Living

– Start your day with a high-fibre breakfast cereal. Oat bran, bran flakes, oatmeal, or one of the new high-fibre breakfast cereals will do. Or, mix a scoop of high-fibre cereal with one of your old favourites. Or, try making your own muesli (recipe page 187).

– Don't miss an opportunity to top up your cereal with a scoop of raisins, a sliced banana, or some orange sections.

– Have a muffin for lunch: make it a bran muffin or an oatmeal muffin. And it's even better if it contains fruit like apples, apricots, raisins or dates (see recipe page 198).

– Add fibre fillers to your meal. Boost your salad with carrots, apple slices, dried fruits, raw broccoli and cauliflower pieces, chick-peas and kidney beans.

– When you have a choice in breads, choose a wholegrain product like wholemeal, rye or mixed grain.

– Load your plate with vegetables. To add a little extra fibre, slice up a fresh tomato . . . put it in your salad, eat it in a sandwich.

– Add some beans and pulses to your meals. For a high-fibre, low-fat meal, try split pea soup (recipe page 44), or baked beans (recipe page 175), with a slice of wholemeal bread and a glass of skimmed milk. Finish up with a piece of fruit.

High-Fibre Eating

This day's menu gives you an idea of how to get the approximate amount of dietary fibre you need each day.

Meal	Fibre
Breakfast	
Apple Juice (4 fl oz/125 ml)	0.4 g
1 Serving (8 fl oz/250 ml) Cooked Oat Bran Cereal	4.0 g
With Milk	0.0 g
Scoop of raisins (2 oz/50 g)	3.5 g
Morning Break	
1 Bran Muffin	2.5 g
Lunch	
Split Pea Soup (8 fl oz/250 ml)	5.4 g
Tuna Sandwich on Wholemeal Bread	
— Bread	2.8 g
— Tuna	0.0 g
Glass of Skimmed Milk (8 fl oz/250 ml)	0.0 g
1 Pear	4.7 g
Dinner	
Baked Chicken Breast (3 oz/75 g)	0.0 g
Baked Potato with Skin	3.5 g
Peas and Carrots Mixed (about 2 oz/50 g peas; 1 carrot)	4.2 g
Salad: Greens and Vegetable Pieces	1.0 g
Glass Skimmed Milk (8 fl oz/250 ml)	0.0 g
Total fibre for the day	**32.0 g**

— Try curried lentils (recipe page 173) in a pitta pocket; have butter beans with your supper.

— Green peas are a very good source of fibre. Add them to whatever you can: casseroles, stir-fried meals, rice or noodles.

— Don't peel potatoes; eat the skin and all!

— Snack on fibre-filled fruits: raspberries, pears, apples, oranges, nectarines and bananas.

— Have a sweet tooth? Some biscuits are quite low in fat and have fibre too. Buy sultana raisin or fig bars; make some low-fat biscuits like Apple Sauce Spice Biscuits (page 206).

Dietary fibre is good for you, but don't overdo it or it may leave you feeling bloated. To help control the gassy part of a high-fibre diet, increase your fibre intake slowly. Also, make sure you drink plenty of fluids, since fibre needs water to work at its best.

DON'T EAT TOO MUCH FAT

This guideline is aimed at getting some fat out of your diet.

Fat and Your Heart

High fat diets, especially diets that are high in saturated fats, tend to raise blood cholesterol levels. As your blood cholesterol goes up, so do your chances of having a heart attack or stroke. **If you could make only one change in your diet, lowering the total amount of fat you eat would be the best action to take.**

A Primer on Dietary Fat

There are different types of fat in food: saturated, monounsaturated and polyunsaturated. Each type has a different effect on your blood cholesterol level.

Although we tend to think of dietary fats as being one type of fat, it is actually a mixture of the three types of fat. However, it's common practice to classify a food according to the type of fat present in the largest amount. For instance, butter is generally referred to as a saturated fat although it contains as much as 30% monounsaturated and 4% polyunsaturated fat.

Saturated fats

These tend to raise blood cholesterol. As a nation we are eating too much saturated fat in proportion to the other food fats, which explains why you are advised to cut down on foods containing saturated fats. Most of the saturated fat you eat comes from animal foods like meat, milk, cheese, butter and lard. However, foods made with hydrogenated vegetable oils like hard margarine and foods containing tropical oils like palm, palm kernel and coconut oil are also high in saturated fats.

Polyunsaturated fats

Can help to lower blood cholesterol. These fats come mostly from vegetable oils like soybean, sunflower and corn oil; nuts like pine nuts, pecans and walnuts. Soft margarines containing over 45% of polyunsaturated fat are a source of these fats. Fish also contains polyunsaturated fat (Omega-3).

Omega-3

These are a type of polyunsaturated fat. Some research indicates that the very long-chain Omega-3 fats found in fish oils may lower blood triglycerides, another type of blood fat also involved in the development of heart disease. Their effect on blood cholesterol is uncertain. Although many people are tempted to supplement their diets with fish oils like cod liver oil, experts advise against this. If you want to increase the amount of Omega-3 fat in your diet, you are advised to eat more fish, as often as two to three times a week.

Monounsaturated fats

May also have a lowering effect on blood cholesterol. These fats come mostly from olive, rapeseed and peanut oil.

Ideally, what you're striving for with healthy eating is to limit your total fat intake to a moderate amount – about 35% of your calories should come from fat.

Although some of the dietary fats described are better in terms of heart health than others, the bottom line is still to limit your total fat intake.

How Much Is Too Much?

Generally we are getting about 40% of calories from fat. We would be healthier if we could reduce this to 35% of calories from fat.

If you're not on a fat-restricted diet and you simply want to eat in a healthier way, there's no need to live with a calculator in hand. However, if you have a general idea of what a healthy fat intake is, it will help you to size up foods and recipes which have been analyzed for fat content.

Approximate Healthy Fat Intake for a Day[1]

Average Woman	65 grams
Average Man	95 grams

Since a healthy fat intake is based on your calorie intake, the amount of fat that is healthy for you may vary with your age and activity level. Younger people or very active people might be able to handle more fat than these amounts; older or less active people may need to eat even less fat than these figures indicate.

Although many foods contain fat, most of the fat you eat will come from five main sources. These are the foods to watch out for:

— butter, margarine, mayonnaise, oil and salad dressings;

— fatty meat and meat products;

— high-fat dairy products like full fat milk, hard cheese, full-fat yogurts; sour cream and ice cream.

— fast foods and snack foods;

— many cakes and biscuits such as croissants and Danish pastries.

Fat-Fighting Ideas

There are all kinds of little ways to cut back on the fat you eat. Added together they can make all the difference that is needed. Here are some fat-fighting ideas for you.

For every teaspoon of butter, margarine and oil you cut out, you save approximately 5 grams of fat. That might be as much as 10 grams of fat it you don't butter your toast or sandwich!

— Buy a good non-stick pan so that you can start foods off with very little or no fat at all. Add a little water if items start to stick to the bottom of the pan. Or use a non-stick cooking spray (such as Fry Light) available from most supermarkets.

— Switch from semi-skimmed milk to skimmed milk and save ½ a gram of fat for every cup you drink[2].

— Although cottage cheese can't compare to hard cheese in calcium content, you could save about 13 grams of fat by eating 4 oz (125 g) of low fat cottage cheese instead of 1½ oz (45 g) of Cheddar cheese. Hard cheeses such as Cheddar cheese, Gloucester, Danish blue usually contain 30% of fat which makes them high in fat.

— Check whether the cheese counter has any lower-fat cheese such as Edam, Jarlsberg or half-fat Cheddar. The selection of half-fat cheeses is growing rapidly and most varieties work well in recipes.

---

[1] Source: Dietary Reference Values for Food Energy and Nutrients for the United Kingdom Department of Heath 1991.

[2] Most of the recipes in this cookbook have been analyzed assuming semi-skimmed milk is used. You can save even more on fat and calories by substituting skimmed milk.

– Use milk in your coffee instead of cream. If you drink 2 to 3 cups of coffee each day, you might save as much as 10 grams of fat.

– Eat smaller servings of meat, fish and poultry. On average, 3½ ounces (90 grams) of a lean cut of meat (beef, pork, lamb) gives you about 9 to 10 grams of fat; poultry without the skin, 5 grams fat; fatty fish like salmon, 7 grams fat, and lean fish like sole, 2 grams fat.

    Ninety grams is approximately a small chicken breast; 1 loin pork chop; 2 loin lamb chops; a slice of meat about the size of a cooked quarter-pound hamburger; a fillet of fish about the length of your outstretched hand and as wide as your three middle fingers.

– Don't spoil the goodness of your salad by dousing it with a high-fat dressing. By using a low-calorie dressing you can reduce your fat intake by up to 12 grams of fat.

– Use lean meat, sliced poultry or canned fish for sandwiches; only use the higher-fat meat products such as sausages, hamburgers and salami occasionally.

– Although fruits and vegetables are generally fat free, the avocado is one exception. One avocado can contain as much as 20 to 30 grams of fat.

– When you go out for a treat, choose a fruit sorbet or a low-fat frozen yogurt instead of ice cream and save yourself at least 12 grams of fat, maybe more.

– When it comes to nibbling, stick to pretzels and homemade popcorn that isn't dripping in fat. Half of a 150 gram bag of crisps gives you about 28 grams of fat.

– Steer clear of cakes, doughnuts, croissants and pies, which rarely contain less that 12 grams of fat.

Cholesterol Facts

Cholesterol, it seems, is always in the news. Trouble is, the information is often more confusing than it is helpful. And that's not good, since keeping your blood cholesterol in a healthy range is important to a healthy heart.

    Although you hear and read about "cholesterol" it would help the understanding of this topic if the cholesterol was identified as either *dietary* or *blood* cholesterol. Cholesterol is a type of fat that is an important part of body cells. It is also a part of some hormones and of bile acids, which help to digest dietary fat.

    Dietary cholesterol is the cholesterol found in foods. Only foods of animal origin contain cholesterol. That's why it's rather silly to label vegetable oils, low in cholesterol since they couldn't possibly contain cholesterol anyway.

    Most people know that eggs contain dietary cholesterol, but so do meat, fish and poultry; foods like biscuits, pies and cakes made with butter or lard; and milk products unless they're made from skimmed milk.

    Although many people believe that the cholesterol in foods is primarily responsible for raising their blood cholesterol, we now know that *dietary* cholesterol doesn't affect *blood* cholesterol nearly as much as dietary *fat* particularly saturated fat. So in terms of healthy eating, the total fat and saturated fat content of your diet deserves your attention far more than dietary cholesterol.[1] **Studies show that when you cut back fat and saturated fat you automatically reduce your dietary cholesterol intake anyway.**

Blood Cholesterol and Tests

This is the cholesterol that gives you the problems. When you've got too much cholesterol in your blood,

---

[1] This advice is intended for those interested in overall healthy eating habits for a family. There is a small percentage of people who have an inherited condition called familial hypercholestrolaemia whose blood cholesterol is much more influenced by dietary cholesterol. Under the care of a doctor and dietitian, these people should restrict dietary cholesterol in addition to keeping dietary fat intake as low as possible.

it can settle on the inside wall of your blood vessels. As it builds up, blood vessels become clogged, the blood can't get through properly and the chances of having a heart attack or stroke are greatly increased.

If you are at particular risk of coronary heart disease your doctor may decide that it is necessary to test your blood cholesterol. The result will give details of your total blood cholesterol level. A level over 5.3 mmol/L (200 mg/dl) is usually considered high although the doctor will take into account your age, whether you smoke and your blood pressure before deciding whether any treatment is necessary.

The Good and The Bad Blood Cholesterol

If a higher proportion of your total cholesterol is HDL (High Density Lipoprotein)[1] cholesterol, that's a good sign – and that's why it's called the "good" cholesterol. HDL cholesterol seems to protect against heart disease by clearing cholesterol from the arteries. People who exercise regularly, non-smokers, pre-menopausal women and moderate drinkers are more likely to have higher HDL cholesterol.

The blood cholesterol that you don't want too much of is the LDL (Low Density Lipoprotein) cholesterol. This "bad" cholesterol is the cholesterol that gets deposited along the arteries, clogging them up and putting you at risk for a heart attack. One of the purposes of healthy eating is to avoid having excessive amounts of LDL cholesterol in your blood stream.

One of the most important ways to keep blood cholesterol at a healthy level is to follow the healthy eating guidelines, making sure you cut down on dietary fat especially saturated fat and increase dietary fibre.

Are Eggs Okay?

Most people can eat eggs in moderation without any harmful rise in blood cholesterol. But what's moderation for normal, healthy people? Three eggs per week? Five eggs per week? Although people seem to want a definite recommendation, there is no magic number.

The best advice is to follow the healthy eating guideline on variety. Just as you shouldn't eat beef every day or ice cream every day, neither should you eat eggs every day.

If your blood cholesterol is really high and it is not coming down as it should, eggs will be restricted to help control both dietary cholesterol and dietary fat intake. Note that it is the egg yolk that contains both the fat and the cholesterol. You can continue to use fresh eggs in most recipes by substituting one or two egg whites for one whole egg.

ENJOYING REGULAR PHYSICAL ACTIVITY AND HEALTHY EATING

The fourth step in our overall plan for healthy eating highlights the fact that good health depends on a healthy body weight, being neither too thin nor too fat but falling within a weight range that is suitable for your particular body build.

From a heart health point of view this is significant because overweight people are at a greater risk of high blood pressure, elevated blood cholesterol, and diabetes, all risk factors for developing heart disease and strokes.

At first, the solution to this problem seems obvious: overweight people should lose weight. However, this is easier said than done.

Experience repeatedly shows that most quick-weight-loss diets fail dismally. And sadly, many diet programmes exploit people by giving them unrealistic hopes for the weight that can be lost, setting them up time and time again for failure. It is estimated that as many as 95% of people who lose weight gain back what they lost. It is clear that diets alone don't work in the long run. That leaves the question: what does work?

---

[1] Lipoproteins are packages of fat and cholesterol wrapped in a shell made partially of protein. They are the means by which fat and fat-related substances can travel in the blood stream.

Weighty Issues

Unfortunately, no one really knows the successful solution for losing weight and keeping it off forever. It seems that efforts should be spent establishing healthy eating and exercise habits early in life so that extra weight never becomes a problem.

For those who are already overweight, the solutions are less clear. Most weight-control experts agree that there is no such thing as an "ideal" body weight. Most people would be healthy within a range of body weights.

The healthy-weight concept helps people to set realistic weight goals for themselves. You can determine just how healthy your weight is through a measurement called the Body Mass Index, or BMI for short.

The BMI is designed for people between 20 and 65 years of age and is considered a fairly accurate way of assessing weight in respect to health. **This measurement should not be used for children, pregnant and nursing women, people older than 65, or highly muscular people.**

What's Your BMI?

Use the following chart to work out your BMI. Once you know your BMI, compare it to the standards below.

Weight Loss for Those Who Need It

There is no magic way to lose weight. If there were, this nation wouldn't have the weight problem it does and all the quick-weight-loss schemes would be out of business. Strict diets don't seem to work. Most health professionals feel that you're more likely to succeed at losing weight by paying close and *equal* attention to these two lifestyle habits.

(1) Eating, not dieting. Of course, what and how much you eat is still important but severely restricted dieting is not the answer. The way to eat is just as described in these healthy-eating guidelines. You want to structure your meals around cereal foods, fruits and vegetables, cutting back on fat and fatty foods, using lower-fat milk products and eating small portions of meat, poultry and fish.

(2) Getting regular physical activity.

Making Sense of Your BMI

BMI less than 20	A BMI of less than 20 may indicate you are underweight. Being underweight is not healthy and can put you at risk for certain health problems. Additional weight loss or struggling to keep your weight at this level would make the problem worse. If, however, this is your natural weight, don't worry; this is a healthy weight for you.
BMI 20-25	Congratulations, you are at a healthy weight already. Keep up the good work through healthy eating and regular physical activity.
BMI 25-30	It's time to sit up and take note. You're not really overweight but it seems that unless you are an athletic or muscular person, you might be headed in that direction. You'll benefit from healthy eating and more physical activity.
BMI over 30	Your weight is high enough to be unhealthy. The more over 30 it is, the greater the health risk for you. Weight loss under medical supervision is recommended.

Are you the right weight for your height?

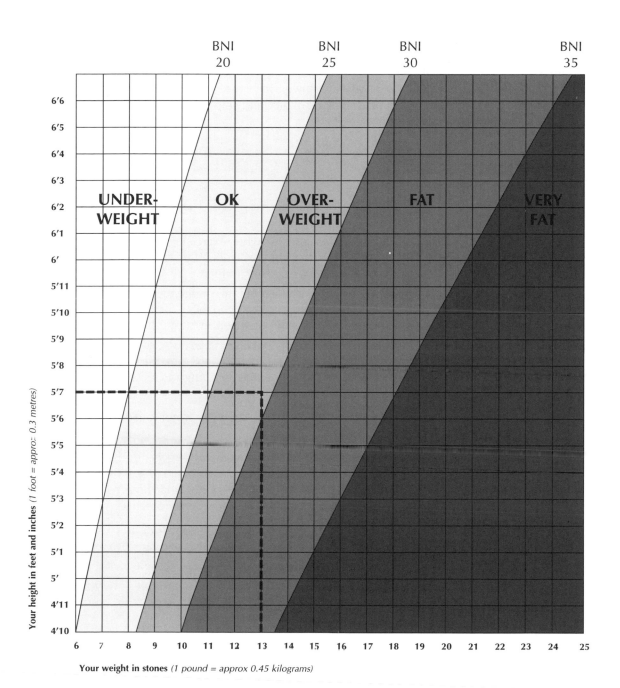

Where Exercise Fits In

There are many weight experts who believe that the condition of being overweight arises not so much because people over-eat but because they under-exercise. In fact, some believe that exercise is one of the best-kept secrets in preventive medicine!

Whatever the cause of being overweight, it is clear that exercise is equally as important as practicing healthy eating habits. Exercise uses up calories, allowing you to eat enough to nourish yourself and feel satisfied, while at the same time helping you to reach and maintain a healthy weight.

In addition, there are other benefits from a heart-health point of view. Regular exercise increases the amount of HDL or "good" cholesterol in your blood. The higher the HDL cholesterol the better, since high levels of this cholesterol are associated with a lower risk of heart disease. Furthermore, exercise helps to control blood pressure, influences smoking habits, and helps you relax and better cope with the stresses and strains of everyday living.

Tips for Putting Exercise Into Your Life

(1) Let the F.I.T.T. principle be your exercise guide.

F stands for FREQUENCY:	Aim to exercise at least every second day, and more often if you're trying to lose weight.
I stands for INTENSITY:	You want to huff and puff while exercising, but you shouldn't push yourself so hard that you can't talk. After years without exercising, start off slowly and build up gradually.
T stands for TIME:	Generally, about a half hour is recommended which includes a 5-minute warm-up to prepare your heart for the extra effort and another 5-minute cool-down period to improve recovery.
T stands for TYPE:	Choose an exercise that involves large muscles: walking, jogging, swimming, bike riding, racquet sports, aerobic dance. Stretching and warming up are good for muscle toning and will help to keep you flexible.

(2) Make an exercise plan outlining what you plan to do, and when you're going to do it. Put it on paper. Make up a progress chart to keep yourself on track.

(3) Choose an activity that you like to do and can do comfortably. Signing up for an advanced aerobics class when you haven't exercised in years can be very frustrating and discouraging. If you're really overweight, try walking or bike riding to begin. Distance is more important than time, so walking a kilometre, even though it takes you longer, is just as beneficial as running a kilometre.

(4) Choose an exercise that is easily incorporated into your daily routine. Walk during your lunch hour; swim if you're near a pool; join the Ramblers; attend an aerobics class that you can go to on the way home from work.

(5) It may be helpful and more fun to exercise in the company of a friend. But don't allow your exercise time to become totally dependent on someone else's schedule. Your goal is to get more exercise every day, whether or not you go with a friend.

LIMIT SALT, ALCOHOL AND CAFFEINE

SALT

We are advised to decrease our intake of salt because it is a major source of sodium, a mineral linked to high blood pressure.

How to Cut Down on Salt

— Try to prepare more foods from scratch instead of relying on packaged convenience foods. Frozen meals, packets of flavoured rice, ready-made sauces, cake mixes and pudding mixes all contain more salt than similar foods made at home from basic ingredients.

— Also watch out for the more processed foods since processing generally results in the use of more salt. For instance, slices of roast meat are lower in salt than processed meat like ham and salami; fresh potatoes don't contain as much salt as instant potatoes; processed cheese food has more salt than hard cheese.

— Watch your consumption of fast food: hamburgers, chicken sandwiches, fish and chips, pizza. These foods are often high in salt.

— Eat fewer snack foods like crisps and salted peanuts, as well as crackers, which can be very high in salt.

— Cut out, or cut by half, the salt called for in recipes.

— Don't add salt to cooking water when cooking vegetables and pasta.

— Use pure seasonings like onion and garlic powder rather than onion and garlic salts for flavouring meats, fish, poultry and vegetables.

— Remove the salt shaker from the table but leave the pepper. A sprinkle of pepper or any favourite spice helps to perk up a food that's crying out for seasoning.

ALCOHOL

Alcohol in moderation is in keeping with a healthy approach to living. More than a moderate intake of alcohol puts you at risk for several health problems including high blood pressure, a major risk factor for stroke and heart disease. Overweight people should also consider the contribution that alcohol makes to their calorie intake.

A moderate intake of alcohol works out to be no more than one to two drinks a day.

What Makes Up a Drink?

- 1 single pub measure[1] (⅙th gill) of spirits, or 1 fl oz (25 ml)

- 1 small glass of sherry or other fortified wine, or 2¾ oz (79 ml)

- 1 small glass of wine, or 4 fl oz (125 ml)

- ½ pint ordinary beer, lager or cider, or 10 fl oz (300 ml)

- ¼ pint strong beer, lager or cider, or 5 fl oz (125 ml)

- 2 small glasses of low alcohol wine, or 8 fl oz (250 ml)

- 1½ pints low alcohol beer, lager or cider, or 30 fl oz (900 ml)

---

[1] Scottish pub spirit measures are 1.2 units.

Tips for Cutting Down

– Cut down the amount of alcohol you drink by mixing alcoholic beverages like wine with sparkling mineral water and beer with lemonade.

– Make every second drink a non-alcoholic drink. Dress up a sparkling mineral water or a tomato juice with a slice of lime.

– Try a low alcohol beer or lager; it can be bought in most supermarkets.

– Drink slowly and enjoy each sip. To avoid over-drinking when you're thirsty, quench your thirst with water before you begin on an alcoholic drink.

– Don't be fooled by your drinks. Beware of the extra strong brews, most are twice as strong as ordinary beer and remember that home measures are usually much more generous.

CAFFEINE AND COFFEE

Sixty percent of the caffeine we consume comes from coffee; 30% of caffeine comes from tea; the remaining 10% comes from three sources: cola beverages; chocolate products, medications. Because so much of the caffeine we consume comes from coffee, it's difficult to separate the effects of caffeine from the effects of other components in the coffee.

Sources of Caffeine

Item		Caffeine
Coffee	6 fl oz (180 ml)	
	Filter drip	110-118 mg
	Instant	60-90 mg
Tea	6 fl oz (180 ml)	
	Weak	20-45 mg
	Strong	79-110 mg
Colas	12 fl oz (375 ml)	
	1 can	22-50 mg
Chocolate products	Chocolate milk 8 oz (250 ml)	2-7 mg
	Chocolate bar 2 oz (56 g)	
	Dark	40-50 mg
	Light	3-20 mg

Are Caffeine and Coffee Safe to Consume?

Although the safety of caffeine and coffee has been questioned many times, there is no convincing evidence linking *moderate* intakes of caffeine or coffee to major health problems. However, higher intakes of caffeine and coffee may have undesirable side effects. Understand, though, that this is still an area of controversy and definite conclusions cannot be drawn.

With these facts in mind, and recognising that the foods containing caffeine are non-nutritious items, we should try to reduce coffee consumption to no more than the equivalent of 4 cups of coffee a day.

That's it for the basic principles of healthy eating listed back on page 1. Now let's look at how we can put these ideas together in specific ways when:

— planning healthy meals and snacks;

— shopping;

— dining out.

PLANNING HEALTHY MEALS

Healthy eating is the sum total of all your meals and snacks. While you should keep the basic rules in mind every time you make or choose a meal, if you break them once in a while this won't do any harm.

Healthy eating doesn't just happen by making a healthy recipe. You're still left with the task of providing a good balance of other food to make up the rest of the meal.

Combining a variety of foods and being sensitive to colour and flavour is the key to planning healthy meals. A good rule of thumb is to combine at least three different kinds of foods as these examples show you.

Sliced roast chicken	(meat)
Brown rice	(grain)
Green beans	(vegetable)
Baked beans	(meat alternative)
Wholemeal roll	(grain)
Glass of skimmed milk	(milk)
Fresh apple	(fruit)
Bran muffin	(grain)
Piece of cheese	(milk)

Planning by the Day and Week

It stands to reason that if every meal is healthy, then each day and week will fall into line. And it would, if life was this easy. But it never is, and there will always be times when meals are far from perfect. That's when some dietary juggling skills come in handy.

For instance, there are bound to be times when you eat more fat than you know is healthy: when you're out for dinner, you're on holidays, or you're preparing a special meal to celebrate something. This is a normal part of life. Healthy eaters can enjoy times like this by planning to compensate for the extra fat at other meals before or after the event. Likewise, frequent travellers often complain about the lack of fibre in restaurant meals. You have to be on the lookout for fibre sources like wholemeal toast and fresh fruit salad. And you may even have to resort to carrying your own fruit along or asking for special foods like raisins for your morning breakfast cereal.

SHOPPING AT ITS BEST

You may cook and eat most meals at home but the chances are that many of your healthy-eating decisions are made as you stand gazing at the thousands of items lining your supermarket shelves. It's one thing to read about healthy eating and quite another to choose the right foods when faced with so many choices when you shop.

In the next few pages you're going to take a supermarket tour, up and down the aisles of a typical supermarket. During this trip, typical items are discussed in terms of healthy eating. Are you ready? Away we go!

Tools of the Trade

Ingredients lists and nutrition information on the labels of packaged food can help you make healthy choices. But they are no substitute for a well-informed shopper. It's up to you to know basic nutrition as discussed in these pages, and to plan for shopping just as you plan your meals. It helps if you have a fairly good idea of what you want to buy before you go to shop. Otherwise, it's easy to be swayed by the glitzy packages and clever sales techniques.

Shopping Savvy

We'll go along the store's outside-wall aisles first, and then head up and down the interior aisles.

- First stop, fresh fruits and vegetables. Load up here, remembering how important variety is. Here's the spot to pick up herbs and spices like garlic and root ginger for low-salt cooking.

- On to fresh meat, poultry and fish. Buy just enough to allow for small (3½ oz/90 g) servings per person. Remember, you're going to try a few meatless meals using beans and pulses.

- Be very selective with the sliced meats as they can be quite high in fat and sodium. Plain roast beef, lean ham or turkey are good choices.

- Buy some fresh eggs; they too can be part of a healthy diet.

- Next stop, the dairy counter, where you pick up milk, yogurt, cottage cheese. Label reading here is essential. The best choices at this counter: semi-skimmed or skimmed milk, low-fat yogurt and cottage cheese.

    When cream or sour cream is needed, look for products with the lowest fat content, or buy plain low-fat yogurt as a substitute for these products.

- On to the cheese counter where you should select some half-fat cheese such as Edam and Jarlsberg.

- Butter or margarine: Healthy eaters use as little of these fats as possible. A good-quality margarine (soft and sold in tubs) will be labelled high in polyunsaturates.

Heading into the interior of the store . . .

- A whole aisle of fizzy drinks and snack foods like crisps and peanuts. Unless your supply of popcorn is low, or you want some mineral water don't even venture into this territory.

- Breakfast cereals: Choose cooked or ready-to-eat, the plain cereals such as oats and Shredded Wheat are nutritious and low in fat. Choose whole grain breakfast cereals when possible. The ones to choose are ones that haven't been sugar-coated. Be careful about some granola-type cereals, which can be high in fat and sugar.

- Jams, marmalade, honey and syrups. While not particularly nutritious, these extras can add life to toast or bread when you're cutting out butter or margarine. Peanut butter is a good meat alternative; it is high in fat but can be used in small amounts.

- Salad dressings: look for low-fat, low-calorie dressings.

— Oils: Choose an oil high in monounsaturated fats, like olive or rapeseed oil, or one high in polyunsaturated fat like soybean, sunflower or corn oil.

— Tea and coffee can still be on your list but heavy coffee drinkers should try to drink less.

— Canned fruit juices are a good choice – don't make the mistake of buying vitamin C enriched *drinks*, which aren't as nutritious as juice. Canned vegetables are generally high in sodium but lower-sodium choices are available. Canned fruits are good too, though they have a little less fibre than fresh; pick ones canned in fruit juice instead of syrup.

— Biscuits and crackers. Most biscuits are high in fat. Good choices are: fruit bars like fig, date and raisin, biscuits like Rich Tea and ginger snaps. Crackers and crispbread: choose varieties that aren't greasy to touch and are lower in salt: melba toast and bread sticks. Watch out for some of the tasty snack crackers, which would be more appropriately sold alongside the crisps.

— Tinned meat and fish: Tuna, salmon, crab, sardines and prawns are good choices; choose water- or salt-varieties when you can. Watch out for salt content if you're on a low salt diet.

— Condiments: Usually high in sodium but useful for flavouring low-fat foods. Look for items like hot honey mustard, salsa sauce, chilli sauce, flavoured vinegars or other low-fat sauces.

— Dried soup and sauce mixes for casseroles are items you can live without – their nutrient content is poor and they are always extremely high in salt.

— On to the deep-freeze where you'll find both good choices and poor choices.

Healthy Choices:	frozen fruit juices; plain frozen vegetables and fruits; frozen bread doughs, French sticks, naans; meats such as lamb or turkey; frozen fish; lower-fat/calorie ready-made meals; sorbet and frozen yogurt.
Not so Healthy Choices:	vegetables in butter sauces; French fries; chips; many ready-made meals; battered and fried meat and fish; cakes; croissants, pastries, ice cream.

— Baking supplies: Here's where you can pick up high-fibre prunes, apricots and raisins and some of the nuts and seeds for sprinkling on meatless meals. Although you'll find coconut and chocolate chips here too, these items shouldn't be regulars in your shopping basket.

— Nuts and dried fruit and small cartons of fresh fruit juice can be handy for snacks and lunch boxes.

— Ethnic foods section: take a good look here. You can often find interesting items such as taco or enchilada shells, tasty sauces, spices, bean- and pulse-based foods like refried beans, which can add variety to your diet.

— Cake mixes and flours: The fewer mixes you can get along with, the better. Scone mix might be one of the few convenience foods to pick up since it is low in fat. Flours: load up, especially if you're going to be making your own low-fat cakes and biscuits. Wholewheat flour is a good choice.

— Canned and dried beans and pulses: Lentils, split peas, chick peas, kidney beans . . . stock up; these are high-fibre, low-fat or no fat foods.

— Pasta and rice: Both are good choices as they are low-fat, high in starch. Try brown rice and wholemeal pasta. Avoid the flavoured rice and pasta meals – very high in salt.

— Tomato and pasta sauces: Great for convenience but high in salt. Try to choose one with a lower salt content. Buy tomato paste and make your own sauce (recipe page 103).

— Breads: try different kinds such as rye, wholemeal, Granary, oatmeal. Look for pitta bread, tortilla, naan and crisp breads.

PACKED LUNCHES AND SNACKS

The planning for packed lunches and snacks is no different from planning meals at home. You're aiming to make the lunch or snack with a variety of nutritious foods.

Lunches to Go

— Nothing invented to date can match the convenience of a sandwich. Use wholemeal bread or rolls but choose different varieties. Go light on mayonnaise and butter/margarine if you use either at all. Pack lettuce and sliced cucumbers or tomatoes separately to be added to the sandwich at lunchtime.

— Pack extra vegetables or fruit to go with a sandwich.

— If you get tired of sandwiches, there's nothing wrong with alternatives like these:
  wholemeal scones/low-fat yogurt/vegetable sticks
  crackers/low-fat cheese/apple
  cottage cheese/sliced pineapple/slice of rye bread
  pasta salad/milk/banana
  slice of pizza/orange

— Stock these foods to add to packed lunches:
  snack-size cheeses
  wholemeal, lower-fat crackers
  small cartons of fruit juices
  individual-sized servings of fruit, yogurt, pudding[1]
  different breads and rolls: pitta bread, bagels, bread pretzels
  low-fat biscuits like Rich Tea, fig bars, sultana raisin biscuits, ginger snaps
  scones
  fruit like bananas, oranges, grapes, apples, pears

— Children are often under a lot of pressure to bring "goodies" in their lunch boxes. Pretzels, homemade popcorn that isn't highly buttered and peanuts or low-fat crisps, once in a while, are good substitutes for crisps as are low-fat biscuits.

Snacks

Snacks should be viewed as just small meals covered by the same principles of healthy eating as regular meals. The food given should be nutritious and safe for teeth. Healthy snacking is particularly important for young children who often get a significant proportion of their day's food from snacks. Here are some suggestions for good snacks:

— semi-skimmed milk, unsweetened fruit juice

— non-sugar-coated breakfast cereals; preferably whole grain

— whole grain crackers with half-fat cheese or peanut butter

---

[1] Individually packaged foods, while convenient, add to the growing problem of rubbish disposal and are not considered environmentally friendly. To be sensitive to environmental issues, consider buying a thermos for each family member and stocking up on a variety of reusable plastic containers and bottles to pack lunches in.

- wholemeal scone or tea cake, not too sweet

- low-fat yogurt

- low-fat milk pudding

- fruit – fresh, or tinned in fruit juice, not syrup

- vegetable sticks or rounds

- bread sticks

- a sandwich

- half bagel with cheese

- slice of pizza

- popcorn or nuts for older children who are less likely to choke on them.

Crisps, cheese biscuits, sweets, cakes, soft drinks and sugared cereals are not good snacks because they are either non-nutritious or their sugar content makes them a poor choice for teeth.

EATING OUT THE HEART HEALTHY WAY

Eating out, especially if it's three or four times a week, can take its toll on an otherwise healthy diet. Restaurant meals tend to be larger, higher in calories, fat and salt and lower in dietary fibre than meals you eat at home. But there's good news too! Now, more than ever before, restaurants are catering to health-conscious customers by offering some healthier menu items.

Here are some tips to help you take advantage of this trend whether you're grabbing a bite or dining out at a five star restaurant

- Go to restaurants, buffets and cafeterias where there is a large and varied menu. When there are lots of different dishes to choose from, you're bound to find some healthy choices.

- Learn to *ask* for what you want: fish that is grilled or baked instead of pan fried; milk for coffee instead of cream, low fat salad dressings and sauces served on the side so you can control the amount that goes on the food.

- Order a vegetable or broth-based soup like chicken noodle instead of a cream soup. Check whether the soup can be served without extra cream.

- Enjoy the fresh bread or rolls without butter or margarine. Always ask for wholemeal or Granary rolls.

- For a main entree, choose low-fat items like a small chicken breast, baked fish, or pasta with a tomato sauce, or a small grilled steak. Old-time favourites like lasagne, quiche and macaroni cheese are fine once in a while but are too high in calories, fat and sodium to choose often.

- Order lower-fat, fibre-rich items like a chilli made with plenty of beans, split pea or minestrone soup; add a wholemeal roll and a glass of semi-skimmed milk or fresh orange juice to complete the meal.

- Watch out for some salads! A green salad and vegetables with a low-fat dressing is a good choice. But salads like potato, pasta and Caesar can be high in calories and fat.

- Choose plain rice or baked potato instead of French fries. The jacket potato can either be eaten on its own or with some low-calorie salad dressing or a sprinkling of pepper, but don't put butter or sour cream on it.

— Try stir-fry meals where you get mostly low-fat rice or pasta, lots of vegetables and little meat. Ask the chef to go light on the oil and stir-fry sauce.

— When portions are large, don't feel that you have to clean your plate if you've had enough.

— Dessert, if eaten at all, should be simple: a fresh fruit salad, sorbet or frozen yogurt.

Fast Foods: How to Get the Best and Leave the Rest

On average, we eat out at least once a week at a fast-food restaurant. But contrary to popular belief, not all fast-food meals are a nutritional disaster. It depends on what you choose.

Fast foods are notoriously high in calories and fat. Deep-fat frying, special sauces and doubling up on cheese and meat are mostly to blame.

How to Cut Down on Calories and Fat

- Always choose the smallest portion size.

- Choose basic menu items like a small hamburger instead of a deluxe burger, a fried chicken or fish sandwich; a small pizza instead of one with extra cheese and pepperoni.

- Order milk or fruit juice instead of a milkshake or fizzy drink.

- Ask for a low-calorie salad dressing to go with salad.

- Beware of breakfast items. A croissant with egg, sausage and bacon is a high-fat way to start your day.

- Give your business to the places that offer healthier menu items: salads, wholemeal bread products, roast beef sandwiches, roast chicken, chilli, bean-based Mexican food.

Fast Food Check

The values for calories and fat are average values for typical fast-food menu items. They are used here to point out that even at fast-food restaurants your choice of food can make a difference.

Fast Food item	Calories	Fat (g)
Small hamburger	260	11
Large burger – 2 burgers, cheese and sauce	950	60
Chicken sandwich	596	33
Fish sandwich	437	26
Bowl of chilli	230	9
Taco	195	11
Green salad with		
– packet light dressing	105	5
– packet regular dressing	262	21
Breakfast sandwich with egg and sausage	435	30

Salt

It's just about impossible to escape high levels of salt in most fast-food meals. Healthy people should try to offset this sodium load at other meals; those on low-salt diets should not east fast foods too often.

Fibre

Dietary fibre is not abundant in most fast-food meals. There are a few fibre-rich items but for the most part, you're going to have to make up for the lack of fibre at other times during the day.

Fibre Finds in Fast Foods

- Salads – Use a low-calorie, low-fat dressing.

- Baked potatoes – Top with something low in calories and fat, like chilli, cottage cheese or salsa instead of bacon and cheese.

- Chilli – The more beans, the better.

- Bean-based Mexican food.

- Wholemeal rolls.

- Wholemeal scones.

- Fruit Salad.

GUIDELINES TO NUTRIENTS

Our rating system is based on the Food Labelling (Amendment) Regulations 1994, which state that if a food (or in this case a recipe) meets 15% of the recommended daily allowance (RDA) of a vitamin or mineral it provides "a source" of that nutrient. If it meets 50% of the RDA it provides an excellent or rich source of that nutrient.

Previous regulations allow a high in polyunsaturates claim to be made as long as the food contains at least 35 grams of fat per 100 grams. In addition at least 45% of the fatty acids must be polyunsaturated fats and not more than 25% of the fatty acids must be saturated fat.

To make a low cholesterol claim the food must contain no more than 5 mg of cholesterol and it must also meet the conditions of the polyunsaturated fat claim.

However there are no regulations for fibre and fat claims but the following guidelines were issued by MAFF in 1993. However because these are only guidelines and not regulations you may find other criteria used due to case law that has developed over a number of years.

Claims Chart

	Low	No Added	Free
Fat	No more than 5 g in either a normal serving of food for which this is more than 100 g or 100 ml or in 100 g or 100 ml of a food for which the normal serving is less than this amount. In the case of a food naturally low in fat the claim must be made in the form "a low fat food".		No more than 0.15 g per 100 g or 100 ml.

	Low	No Added	Free
Saturates	No more than 3 g in either a normal serving of a food for which this is more than 100 g or 100 ml *or* in 100 g or 100 ml of a food for which the normal serving is less than this amount. In the case of a food naturally low in saturates the claim must be made in the form "a low saturates food".		No more than 0.1 g per 100 g or 100 ml.
Sugar(s)	No more than 5 g in either a normal serving of a food for which this is more than 100 g or 100 ml *or* in 100 g or 100 ml of a food for which the normal serving is less than this amount. In the case of a food naturally low in sugar(s) the claim must be made in the form "a low sugar(s) food".	No sugars or foods composed mainly of sugars added to the food or to any of its ingredients.	No more than 0.2 g per 100 g or 100 ml.
Salt/Sodium	No more than 40 mg in either a normal serving of a food for which this is more than 100 g or 100 ml *or* in 100 g or 100 ml of a food for which the normal serving is less than this amount. In the case of a food naturally low in salt/sodium the claim must be made in the form "a low salt/sodium food".	No salts or sodium shall have been added to the food or to any of its ingredients.	No more than 5 mg per 100 g or 100 ml.
Fibre	Either 3 g per 100 g or 100 ml *or* at least 3 g in the reasonable expected daily intake of the food. In the case of a food naturally high in fibre, the claim must take the form "a high fibre food".	At least 25% more than a similar food for which no claim is made *and* at least 3 g in either the reasonable daily intake of a food for which this is lower than 100 g or 100 ml *or* in 100 g or 100 ml.	Either at least 6 g per 100 g or 100 ml *or* at least 6 g of the reasonably expected daily intake of the foods.

Government Guidelines for Percentage of Daily Total Energy/Calorie Intake

	Individual minimum	Population average	Individual maximum
Total fat		33 (35)	
Saturated fat		10 (11)	
Polyunsaturates	n – 3 0.2 n – 6 1.0	6 (6.5)	10
Monounsaturates		12 (13)	
Trans fatty acids		2 (2)	
Total carbohydrate		47 (50)	
Free sugars	0	10 (11)	
Fibre	20 g/day	30 g/day	40 g/day

* The figures in brackets are for those people who do not drink alcohol, which on average accounts for 5% of food intake

Nutrient analysis was done using cup and imperial measurements by Info Access using CBORD software system with the Canadian Nutrient File (1988). However additional information in the book has been provided by McCance and Widdowson "The Composition of Foods" and manufacturers' data.

Unless otherwise stated, all recipes in the book were tested using low-fat yogurt, half-fat cottage cheese, semi-skimmed milk, soft margarine and rapeseed oil. As well, most of the recipes in the book do not have added salt, or include salt to taste, therefore they have been analysed without, or using a minimum of, salt.

Nutrient analysis is based on the first ingredient listed when a choice is given and does not include any optional ingredients. The numbers have been rounded off.

There you have it: everything you need to know about light-hearted healthy eating. Why not make a point of trying at least one of these recipes every single day?

Appetizers and Snacks

Oriental Salad Rolls

Skewered Tortellini

Spinach and Artichoke Dip

Tomato Bruschetta with
Fresh Basil

Chicory with Chèvre and
Prawns

Light and Easy Guacamole

Spring Onion Dip

Smoked Salmon Spread

Mexican Bean Dip

Tomato and Cucumber Salsa

Spicy Chicken Skewers

Thai Peanut Sauce

Cheesy Chilli Quesadillas

Quick Mexican Burritos

Quick Tomato, Broccoli and
Red Onion Pizza

Citrus Sangria

Gazpacho Cooler

Oriental Salad Rolls

Perfect for a first course, because they can be prepared in advance, these wonderfully flavoured rolls look and taste terrific. Rice paper wrappers (usually from Thailand) are available at some specialty food shops and at Chinese supermarkets. Add more crushed chillies to taste depending on how hot you like your food.

Sauce

4 fl oz	rice vinegar	125 ml
2 tbsp	soy sauce	30 ml
2 tbsp	hoisin sauce	30 ml
1 tbsp	peanut butter	15 ml
2 tsp	granulated sugar	10 ml
1 tsp	grated fresh ginger root	5 ml
⅛ tsp	crushed chillies	0.5 ml

Rolls

2 oz	rice noodles (rice vermicelli)	50 g
8	shiitake mushrooms (fresh or dried)	8
4 tbs	chicken or vegetable stock	60 ml
8	small spring onions, trimmed	8
16	rice paper wrappers (8 in/20 cm rounds)	16
8	leaves Butterhead lettuce, halved	8
2 oz	bean sprouts	50 g
2	small carrots, coarsely grated	2
2 tbsp	each fresh mint and coriander leaves	30 ml

Sauce: In small bowl, combine rice vinegar, soy sauce, hoisin sauce, peanut butter, sugar, ginger and crushed chillies.

Rolls: In a pan of boiling water, cook noodles for 2 minutes; drain and cool under cold water. Drain and transfer to bowl. Pour 4 tbs (60 ml) of the sauce over noodles and mix well; set aside.

Soak dried mushrooms (if using) in hot water until soft; cut into thin strips. In small saucepan, cook mushrooms in chicken stock for 3 minutes or until tender. Cut spring onions lengthwise into thin strips; cut into 3 in (8 cm) lengths.

In a large bowl of hot water, soak 1 round of rice paper wrapper for 2 minutes or until softened. Remove from water, place on work surface and fold in half.

Right:
Chicory with Chèvre and Prawns (page 31), Skewered Tortellini (page 25), Smoked Salmon Spread (page 34), Spinach and Artichoke Dip (page 26)

PER SERVING (of 2 each)	
calories	77
g total fat	1
g saturated fat	trace
g fibre	1
g protein	3
g carbohydrate	16
mg cholesterol	0
mg sodium	187
mg potassium	162
Excellent: vitamin A	

Place lettuce leaf on wrapper with top of lettuce extending slightly over folded half of wrapper. Place a few slices of spring onion on top to extend over wrapper slightly. Top with spoonful of noodles, then 2 mushroom pieces, a few bean sprouts, carrots, mint and coriander.

Fold up rounded edge of wrapper, then roll wrapper around filling. Repeat with remaining wrappers. (Rolls can be covered and refrigerated for up to 6 hours.)

Serve 2 rolls per person on individual plates. Pass remaining sauce (for dipping) separately. Makes 8 servings.

Skewered Tortellini

Tortellini or capeletti filled with meat or cheese fillings are easy to skewer and make a fabulous appetizer. Buy different coloured pasta to thread onto wooden skewers, then arrange them on a platter along with crudités and a dip such as Spinach and Artichoke on page 26.

PER SKEWER	
calories	35
g total fat	2
g saturated fat	trace
g fibre	trace
g protein	1
g carbohydrate	4
mg cholesterol	2
mg sodium	22
mg potassium	16

8 oz	tortellini or capeletti*	225 g
1 tbsp	olive oil	15 ml

In a large pan of boiling water, cook tortellini according to directions on the packet or until pasta is tender but firm. Drain and return to the pan, toss with oil to prevent sticking.

Thread 2 tortellini, 1 of each colour, onto a skewer. (Skewers can be covered and refrigerated for up to 1 day.) To serve, bring tortellini to room temperature or reheat by dipping into boiling water. Makes about 25 skewers.

*Available in chilled food and ready-made meal sections in most supermarkets.

Left:
Tomato Bruschetta with Fresh Basil (page 27)
Quick Tomato, Broccoli and Red Onion Pizza (page 40)

Stuffed Cherry Tomatoes
Slice the top off cherry tomatoes and scoop out seeds; fill with Smoked Salmon Spread (page 34) or with Spinach and Artichoke Dip.

I don't add yogurt before combining the ingredients in the food processor because when processed, the yogurt breaks down and becomes less thick.

Spinach and Artichoke Dip

Serve this tasty dip with fresh vegetables or with the Tortellini Skewers on page 25. Or halve the amount of yogurt and use as a stuffing for mushrooms, cherry tomatoes, celery or chicory leaves and garnish with a strip of sun-dried tomatoes.

10 oz	frozen chopped spinach	275 g
1	jar (11 oz/285 g) artichoke hearts, drained	1
3 oz	reduced calorie or light mayonnaise	75 g
1 tbsp	chopped fresh dill or basil or ½ tsp dried	15 ml
1	small garlic clove, chopped	1
12 oz	low-fat yogurt	350 g
	salt and pepper	

Thaw spinach and squeeze dry. In food processor, process spinach and artichokes until coarsely chopped. Add mayonnaise, dill or basil, and garlic; process until mixed.

Stir in yogurt. Season with salt and pepper to taste. (Dip can be covered and refrigerated for up to 24 hours.) If too thick add more yogurt. Makes about 1¼ pints (750 ml).

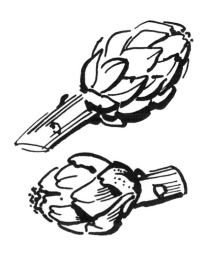

PER TBSP (15 ml)	
calories	14
g total fat	1
g saturated fat	trace
g fibre fat	trace
g protein	1
g carbohydrate	1
mg cholesterol	2
mg sodium	32
mg potassium	42

Tomato Bruschetta with Fresh Basil

We make this often for lunch or a snack, especially on the weekends in August or September when tomatoes are sweet and juicy. If fresh basil isn't available, use 1 tsp (5 ml) dried and sprinkle with 2 tbsp (30 ml) grated Parmesan, or dot with soft chèvre and grill for 1 minute.

2	large tomatoes, diced (about 1 ¼ lb/500 g)	2
4 tbsp	chopped fresh basil, lightly packed	60 ml
1	garlic clove, finely chopped	1
	salt and pepper	
½	French loaf or Italian bread or 1 French baguette	½
1	large garlic clove, halved	1
1 tbsp	olive oil	15 ml
2 tbsp	freshly grated Parmesan cheese (optional)	30 ml

In a bowl, combine tomatoes, basil, garlic and salt and pepper to taste; leave to stand for 15 minutes or cover and refrigerate for up to 4 hours.

Slice bread in 1 in (2.5 cm) thick slices. Place on a baking sheet and grill until lightly browned on each side. Rub cut side of garlic clove over one side of bread; brush with olive oil. Spoon tomato mixture over top. Sprinkle with Parmesan (optional). If tomato mixture has been refrigerated, grill bruschetta for 1 minute. Makes about 16 slices.

PER SLICE	
calories	64
g total fat	1
g saturated fat	trace
g fibre	1
g protein	2
g carbohydrate	11
mg cholesterol	1
mg sodium	105
mg potassium	70

Children and Healthy Eating

Parents, it's up to you to lay the foundation for good eating habits: your children will follow your example. To make it easier, here are some tips and techniques on feeding your children. And, best of all, good nutrition also means delicious-tasting food – please, enjoy your mealtimes together.

Tips to help establish good eating habits in children:

— Set a good example yourself and children will usually follow.

— Remember, you are in control: pre-school children don't usually go shopping by themselves, so if junk food isn't in the house, you have solved half the problem.

— Be positive at mealtimes. Don't give any attention to children who are fussing over their food or not eating. Do give attention to the child who eats a variety of foods. Usually this works best when handled subtly. For instance, talk about how good a certain food tastes, rather than pointing out the child who is eating it. The child who isn't eating it not only doesn't get any attention but is left out of the conversation.

— Serve food that tastes good. Young children usually like their food quite plain and not overly seasoned or sauced.

— Don't bribe, plead or let the children think they have a hold over you by what they eat – they will quickly take advantage of it.

— Be sensible. If you give small children biscuits just before dinner, they won't be as hungry at dinner. If they are screaming with hunger, consider feeding them earlier or at least give them a nutritious snack of raw carrots, apple wedges, or half a slice of wholemeal bread.

— Don't try to sell food to children by telling them it is good for them – they don't care. Sell it because it tastes good. Discuss good eating habits and point out that we need a variety of food. This is best done when children are enjoying their food, not when they're fussing.

— Don't give up when introducing new foods to children. They might not like the food the first time they eat it, but often children like the food by the second or third try. It's best to introduce new foods one at a time along with familiar foods, such as a new vegetable in a stew or vegetable soup.

— Serve small portions to small children – although you're responsible for serving the right kinds of food, let the children decide how much they can eat. Just as adults are hungrier some days, so are children.

— Find out what snacks or meals are served and eaten at school or daycare; keep this in mind when planning your meals.

Tips for packing a nutritious lunch children will love:

— Involve children in making lunches instead of giving them money to spend on chips and fizzy drinks. Now that my children are teenagers I often give them money for the supermarket to choose their own lunch. This way they can choose foods they like.

— Tell children that a good lunch has a choice from each of the four food groups:
    dairy (yogurt, milk, cheese)
    fruits and vegetables
    wholemeal bread and other starchy foods
    meats or alternatives.
If children choose foods they like from these groups, it is more likely the lunch will be eaten and not thrown away.

- Choose wholemeal, rye or pumpernickel instead of white bread. And choose wholemeal scones or wholemeal pitta or rolls, not only for extra fibre but also for taste.

- Vary sandwich fillings; include sliced cold meat leftovers from dinner, sliced turkey or chicken, half-fat cheese, salmon or peanut butter. Choose tuna that has been packed in water, not oil.

- Omit butter or margarine or use as little as possible; choose reduced calorie or light mayonnaise and add lettuce, alfalfa sprouts, grated carrots, sliced cucumber or tomato for flavour and to keep the sandwich from drying out. (Pack the juicier items like cucumber, tomato or lettuce separately to add at the last minute or the sandwich may be too soggy to eat.)

- Pack raw vegetables along with a dip (one of the easiest ways to get children to eat vegetables). See the Mexican Bean Dip recipe on page 35 or the Spring Onion Dip on page 33.

- Pack a safe lunch. My children freeze the small juice boxes (if your freezer is very cold, put the frozen boxes in the refrigerator the night before). By lunchtime they will be thawed but still cold and will have kept the rest of the lunch cool. If you have a soft insulated lunch bag and a frozen juice box, you can safely pack yogurt or cottage cheese.

- Choose foods that keep safely at room temperature. In warm weather, cheese and peanut butter are good choices; avoid eggs, fish and poultry.

- Don't reuse lunch box wrappings; they may contain bacteria.

- Use leftovers for lunch. Pizza, stir frys, pasta dishes, meatloaf, bean salad and coleslaw make good lunch choices.

- Include a hot lunch by using a wide-necked thermos flask to hold chilli, baked beans, spaghetti with meat sauce, soups or stew.

- Include a nutritious sweet such as Easy Date and Walnut Squares (recipe page 205), Pineapple Carrot Bars (recipe page 204), oatmeal biscuits, Cinnamon Carrot Bread (recipe page 194), pudding or applesauce.

Snacks

Snacks are an important part of children's diet and need to be chosen carefully. Whether a snack is bought or homemade, avoid ones that are high in fat and sugar. This doesn't mean children can never have a bag of crisps, but they shouldn't be eaten daily. Try to keep a supply of good-for-you foods that children can eat such as fruit, raw vegetables or yogurt.

- Toast half a wholemeal roll, top with a tomato slice or spread with tomato sauce and half-fat Cheddar-style cheese. Sprinkle with oregano and microwave until the cheese melts.

- Use wholemeal pitta bread as a base for mini pizzas or tear a pitta into pieces and dip into hummus (chick-pea dip) or the Mexican Bean Dip (recipe page 35).

- Top half a Granary roll with ricotta cheese and chopped fresh dill or apple slices; or peanut butter and sliced banana; or light soft cheese and sliced cucumber.

- Keep low-fat or fruit-flavoured yogurt on hand, mix with fresh fruit or chopped dried fruits or low-sugar cereals.

- Spread small flour tortillas with refried beans or chopped tomato or chopped cooked chicken; add grated half-fat cheese; roll up and microwave until cheese melts.

Comparisons of Snack Foods

	calories	g fat	sodium
Popcorn ½ oz (15 g), plain	23	trace	0
Popcorn, ½ oz (15 g) with 1 tsp (5 ml) oil, plus salt	68	5	233
Popcorn, ½ oz (15 g) with sugar coating	142	1	0
Mixed nuts, 1 oz (25 g) dry roasted	197	17	4
oil roasted plus salt	210	19	222
Potato crips (10)	105	7	94
Pretzels, bread-stick (5)	59	trace	252
Doughnut	174	11	98
Chocolate Chip biscuits	103	6	70
Milk chocolate bar (30 g)	156	10	28
Ice cream, 4 oz (125 g)	142	8	61
Frozen fruit yogurt – 4 oz (125 g)	148	5	63
Fruit yogurt, 4 oz (125 g)	131	2	81
Apple	84	0	0
Banana	105	0	1

Comparing Hamburgers
Healthy eating doesn't necessarily mean giving up your favourite foods but making choices. All burgers are not equal: the beef we buy, how we cook it, and what we put on it can make a big difference in the amount of fat.

Standard:
Regular mince (3 oz/75 g) beef burger, fried with a white roll, 2 tsp (10 ml) butter or margarine, 1 tbsp (15 ml) relish or ketchup and 1 slice (1 oz/25 g) processed cheese = 56% calories from fat.

Healthier choice (less fat, high in fibre):
Lean mince (3 oz/75 g) beef burger, grilled with wholemeal roll, 1 slice tomato, 1 piece lettuce, chopped onion and 1 tbsp (15 ml) relish = 34% calories from fat.

Chicory with Chèvre and Prawns

This easy-to-prepare appetizer looks very fancy and tastes terrific. It's my daughter Susie's favourite. Serve on a large platter along with cherry tomatoes.

4	chicory heads	4
5 oz	soft chèvre (goat) cheese	150 g
5 tbsp	ricotta cheese	75 ml
	pepper	
4 oz	small cooked prawns	125 g
	small sprigs fresh dill (optional)	

Divide chicory into individual leaves; wash under cold running water and drain well.

In a small bowl, combine chèvre, ricotta and pepper to taste; mix well.

Fill wide end of each chicory leaf with cheese mixture; top with prawns. Garnish with sprig of dill (if using).

Makes about 30 appetizers.

PER CHICORY	
calories	23
g total fat	1
g saturated fat	1
g fibre	trace
g protein	2
g carbohydrate	1
mg cholesterol	10
mg sodium	64
mg potassium	19

Avocado and Asparagus Guacamole
When asparagus is in season try this delicious variation: instead of peas, substitute 8 oz (225 g) cooked asparagus.

Light and Easy Guacamole

Because avocado is high in fat, I use a mixture of green peas and avocado and still have the authentic flavour of a traditional Mexican dip. Serve with crudités, Chicory leaves or baked tortilla chips.

8 oz	frozen peas, thawed	225 g
1	avocado, peeled	1
2	large tomatoes, peeled, seeded and chopped	2
2	small garlic cloves, finely chopped	2
½	small red onion, finely chopped	½
2 tbsp	fresh lemon juice	30 ml
1 tsp	chilli powder	5 ml
½ tsp	each salt and ground cumin	2.5 ml
Pinch	cayenne pepper	Pinch

In a food processor, purée peas until smooth. In a bowl, mash avocado with a fork; add peas, tomatoes, garlic, onion, lemon juice, chilli powder, salt, cumin and cayenne pepper; mix until blended. Makes approx 1 pint (600 ml).

PER 2 TBSP (30 ML)	
calories	41
g total fat	2
g saturated fat	trace
g fibre	1
g protein	1
g carbohydrate	5
mg cholesterol	0
mg sodium	99
mg potassium	166

Fresh Basil Dip
Prepare Spring Onion Dip, but add ½ oz (15 g) chopped fresh basil to blender.

Spring Onion Dip

My children love this dip with fresh vegetables. I like to add fresh basil or any other fresh herbs that I have on hand.

8 oz	low-fat cottage cheese	225 g
4 tbsp	chopped spring onions	60 ml
4 tbsp	chopped fresh parsley	60 ml
5 oz	low-fat yogurt	150 g
	salt and pepper	

In a blender or processor, process cottage cheese, onions and parsley. Transfer to bowl and stir in yogurt. Season with salt and pepper to taste. Cover and refrigerate for 1 hour or up to 2 days. Makes approx 12 fl oz (350 ml).

PER 2 TBSP (30 ML)	
calories	24
g total fat	trace
g saturated fat	trace
g fibre	trace
g protein	3
g carbohydrate	2
mg cholesterol	2
mg sodium	84
mg potassium	54

Choose carefully when you buy cheese and crackers for a snack. Better choices for crackers are melba toast, rice cakes, crisp breads and water biscuits. Crackers made with fat or cheese are much higher in fat. Compare: 2 Ryvita with 4 tbsp (60 ml) 2% cottage cheese have 2 g fat; 4 Ritz crackers with 2 tbsp (30 ml) cream cheese have 15 g fat.

Smoked Salmon Spread

Spread this creamy mixture on melba toast or use it to stuff mushrooms, cherry tomatoes or chicory leaves. Smoked trout can be used instead of salmon.

8 oz	ricotta cheese	225 g
2 oz	smoked salmon, chopped	50 g
2 tbsp	chopped fresh dill	30 ml
2 tbsp	drained capers	30 ml
2 tsp	lemon juice	10 ml
2 tsp	tomato ketchup	10 ml
1 tsp	prepared horseradish	5 ml
	salt and pepper	

In a food processor or blender, purée ricotta until smooth. Add smoked salmon, dill, capers, lemon juice, ketchup and horseradish; using pulse button, process until lightly mixed. Season with salt and pepper to taste. Makes 11 fl oz (325 ml).

PER TBSP (15 ML)	
calories	22
g total fat	1
g saturated fat	1
g fibre	0
g protein	2
g carbohydrate	1
mg cholesterol	5
mg sodium	189
mg potassium	24

Children's Lunch Menu
*Mexican Bean Dip with Raw
Carrots, Celery and Green
Peppers
Wholemeal Crackers
Slice of Cheese
Orange Sections
Oatmeal Biscuit*

Canned refried beans can be
found in the Mexican food
section of most supermarkets.
Or, you can use canned pinto
beans, drained and rinsed, then
mashed with a chopped tomato
and 1 tsp (5 ml) of cumin.

PER 2 TBSP (30 ML)	
calories	35
g total fat	trace
g saturated fat	trace
g fibre	2
g protein	2
g carbohydrate	6
mg cholesterol	0
mg sodium	126
mg potassium	137

PER 2 TBSP (30 ML)	
calories	4
g total fat	trace
g saturated fat	0
g fibre	trace
g protein	trace
g carbohydrate	1
mg cholesterol	0
mg sodium	1
mg potassium	42

Mexican Bean Dip

Children love this as a filling for celery, as a dip with vegetables, or
as a sandwich spread along with lettuce, sliced tomato or
cucumber inside pitta rounds. Fresh or canned chillies (hot or mild)
are also delicious in this dip. For a party, sprinkle it with shredded
Cheddar cheese.

1	can (15.2 oz/432 g) refried beans	1
5 tbsp	low-fat yogurt	75 ml
2	spring onions, chopped	2
1	garlic clove, finely chopped	1
1 tsp	each cumin and chilli powder	5 ml
2 tbsp	chopped fresh coriander or parsley	30 ml

In a bowl, combine beans, yogurt, onions, garlic, cumin and
chilli powder; mix well. Cover and refrigerate for up to 2 days.
Just before serving, sprinkle with parsley or coriander. Makes
about 1 pt (600 ml).

Tomato and Cucumber Salsa

Serve this with tacos or burritos or as a dip.

1	large tomato, finely diced	1
½	cucumber, finely diced	½
1	small green chilli pepper (canned or fresh), chopped or ¼ tsp (1 ml) crushed chillies	1
2 tbsp	onion, finely chopped	30 ml
1 tbsp	wine vinegar	15 ml
1 tbsp	chopped fresh coriander (optional)	15 ml
½	garlic clove, chopped	½

In a bowl, combine tomato, cucumber, chilli pepper, onion,
vinegar, coriander (if using) and garlic; mix well.
Transfer 8 fl oz (250 ml) of the tomato mixture to food processor,
or blender and purée; return to remaining mixture in bowl. Serve
at room temperature within 3 hours or cover and refrigerate for up
to 3 days. Makes about 1 pt (600 ml).

PER SKEWER	
calories	15
g total fat	trace
g saturated fat	trace
g fibre	0
g protein	2
g carbohydrate	trace
mg cholesterol	6
mg sodium	15
mg potassium	20

Spicy Chicken Skewers

Nice for a summer barbecue or a winter cocktail party, serve these mouthfuls of spicy tender chicken as an hors d'oeuvre, or cut into long strips as a main course. For a satay, serve with Thai Peanut Sauce (recipe follows). For a less spicy version, reduce or omit crushed chillies.

1 lb	boneless skinless chicken fillets or breasts	450 g
Marinade		
2 tbsp	cider vinegar	30 ml
2 tbsp	dry sherry	30 ml
2 tbsp	runny honey	30 ml
2 tbsp	soy sauce	30 ml
2 tbsp	fresh root ginger, finely chopped	30 ml
1 tbsp	sesame oil	15 ml
1 tsp	ground coriander	5 ml
1	large garlic clove, finely chopped	1
½ tsp	crushed chillies	2.5 ml

Cut chicken into very thin ½ in (1 cm) wide strips about 2 in (5 cm) long (for appetizers) or 5 in (12 cm) long for main course.

Marinade: In a bowl, combine vinegar, sherry, honey, soy sauce, ginger, sesame oil, coriander, garlic and chillies; mix well. Add chicken and stir to coat. Cover and refrigerate for 2 hours or up to 24 hours.

Meanwhile, soak 48 toothpicks or 24 wooden skewers in water for 30 minutes. Remove chicken from marinade and thread onto toothpicks or skewers.

Place on baking sheet and grill for 2 minutes on each side or until no longer pink inside. Makes 48 hors d'oeuvres or 4 main-course servings.

PER MAIN COURSE SERVING	
calories	175
g total fat	5
g saturated fat	1
g fibre	trace
g protein	26
g carbohydrate	6
mg cholesterol	70
mg sodium	183
mg potassium	242
Excellent: niacin	

Thai Peanut Sauce

Use this hot Thai sauce for dipping Spicy Chicken Skewers (facing page) or with your favourite satay recipe. This isn't a low-fat recipe; however, it is lower in fat than most peanut sauces. Because it's hot and spicy, you'll probably want just a little.

6 oz	dry-roasted unsalted peanuts*	175 g
½ pt	water	300 ml
3	garlic cloves	3
2 tbsp	soft brown sugar	30 ml
2 tbsp	fresh lime juice	30 ml
1 tbsp	soy sauce	15 ml
¼ tsp	crushed chillies	1.5 ml
1	piece (1 in/2.5 cm) fresh root ginger, peeled and thinly sliced	1

In a blender or food processor, combine peanuts, water, garlic, sugar, lime juice, soy sauce, chillies and fresh root ginger; process for 2 minutes. Pour into the top of a double boiler over boiling water; cook for 2 minutes, stirring occasionally. (Sauce can be covered and refrigerated for up to 2 weeks.) Serve warm. Makes about 1 pt (600 ml).

* To roast peanuts: place on baking sheet and roast in 350°F (180°C) Gas Mark 4 oven for 12 minutes.

PER TBSP (15 ML)	
calories	30
g total fat	2
g saturated fat	trace
g fibre	0
g protein	1
g carbohydrate	2
mg cholesterol	0
mg sodium	16
mg potassium	37

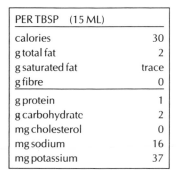

Baked Quesadillas
Prepared as below except bake on baking sheet in 375°F (190°C) Gas Mark 5 oven for 10 minutes or until crisp.

Cheesy Chilli Quesadillas

A quesadilla (pronounced Kay-sa-dee-a) is a turnover made with a Mexican tortilla and usually filled with cheese plus other optional fillings such as ham, cooked chicken or sausage, green chillies or refried beans. It's then topped with salsa or taco sauce to make a great snack, lunch or light supper.

4	soft 8 in (20 cm) flour or corn tortillas	4
4 oz	half-fat cheddar cheese or mozzarella cheese, grated	125 g
2 oz	chopped canned green chillies	50 g
4 tbsp	chopped spring onions	60 ml
2 tsp	vegetable oil	10 ml
	Tomato and Cucumber Salsa (page 35)	
	shredded lettuce	

Sprinkle half of each tortilla with cheese, chillies and onions. Fold tortillas in half and press edges together.

Brush a non-stick frying pan with 1 tsp (5 ml) of the oil; heat over medium-high heat. Cook 2 of the tortillas for about 4 minutes on each side or until golden and cheese melts. Remove from heat; cut into 3 wedges. Repeat with remaining tortillas. Top with Tomato and Cucumber Salsa and shredded lettuce. Makes 4 servings.

PER SERVING (1 TORTILLA)	
calories	198
g total fat	8
g saturated fat	3
g fibre	1
g protein	10
g carbohydrate	21
mg cholesterol	17
mg sodium	330
mg potassium	129
Good: vitamin C, niacin, calcium Excellent: vitamin A	

When shopping for cheeses, look for those with the lowest fat content. Cheese that is "low fat" (reduced fat) or "half fat" will have a fat content 15% or less, about 4.5 g fat per oz (25 g). Skimmed milk cheese has 7% b.f. or less, or about 2.1 g fat per oz (25 g). By comparison, regular cheddar cheese has 32% fat per 100 g or about 9.6 g fat per oz (25 g).

In recipes that call for grated, chopped, or crumbled cheddar or other hard cheese, remember that 1 oz (25 g) solid cheese equals about 4 tbsp (60 ml) grated cheese.

Quick Mexican Burritos

This is the way my children make burritos. They spread the tortillas with mashed beans, top with grated cheese and chopped vegetables or salsa, then roll up to bake or microwave.

1	can (15.2 oz/432 g) refried beans	1
5 tbsp	salsa or water	75 ml
4	9 in (23 cm) flour tortillas	4
1	medium tomato, chopped	1
4	small spring onions, chopped	4
½	green pepper, chopped (optional)	½
4 oz	half-fat cheddar cheese, grated	125 g
	shredded lettuce	
	Salsa (pages 35 or 190) or taco sauce	
	Greek-style yogurt or low-fat yogurt	

Combine beans and salsa or water; mix well.

Thinly spread about 5 tbsp (75 ml) bean mixture over each tortilla, leaving 1 in (2.5 cm) border. Sprinkle tomato, spring onions, green pepper (if using) and half the cheese over tortillas.

Roll up each tortilla and place, seam side down, in lightly greased baking dish. Bake in 400°F (200°C) Gas Mark 6 oven for 10 minutes. Sprinkle with remaining cheese; bake for 5 minutes longer or until heated through and cheese melts. (Alternatively, cover with greaseproof paper and microwave on Medium-high (70%) power for 2 to 4 minutes or until heated through.)

Serve each burrito on a bed of shredded lettuce. Serve salsa or taco sauce and sour cream or yogurt separately. Makes 4 servings.

PER SERVING	
calories	308
g total fat	8
g saturated fat	3
g fibre	8
g protein	17
g carbohydrate	43
mg cholesterol	17
mg sodium	655
mg potassium	699
Good: vitamin A, riboflavin Excellent: vitamin C, calcium, iron, niacin	

Pizza

Pizza makes a great snack or a quick supper. You can make your own great-tasting pizza in less time than it takes to have one delivered. You'll save money as well!

Pick up ready-made pizza crusts at any supermarket or keep them on hand in the refrigerator or freezer. Or, buy ready-made pizza dough, either fresh or frozen, for when you have the time to roll it out. For other quick crusts, you could also use pitta bread rounds or make pizza using French bread halved lengthwise.

Use your favourite toppings or the ones suggested here; they take only seconds to prepare. Vegetable toppings add fibre, vitamins and minerals. Avoid salty or higher fat toppings, such as anchovies, olives, bacon, pepperoni and high-fat cheese.

Quick Tomato, Broccoli and Red Onion Pizza

Juicy vegetable toppings make a pleasing combination of flavours.

1	12 in (30 cm) pizza crust	1
4 tbsp	tomato sauce*	60 ml
1½ tsp	dried oregano	7.5 ml
½	green pepper, chopped	½
1	medium tomato, sliced	1
2 oz	small broccoli florets	50 g
1	red onion, thinly sliced into rings	1
2 tbsp	chopped fresh basil or ¼ tsp (1.5 ml) dried	30 ml
4 oz	half-fat cheddar cheese or mozzarella cheese, grated	125 g
Pinch	crushed chillies (optional)	Pinch

Place pizza crust on non-stick baking sheet or pizza pan. Spread tomato sauce over crust; sprinkle with oregano.

Arrange green pepper, tomato, broccoli, onion and basil over sauce. Sprinkle with cheese, then crushed chillies (if using). Bake in 450°F (230°C) Gas Mark 8 oven for 10 minutes or until cheese is bubbly. Makes 4 servings.

* To reduce sodium: Instead of tomato sauce, use 2 tbsp (30 ml) tomato purée mixed with 4 tbsp (60 ml) water.

PER SERVING	
calories	205
g total fat	7
g saturated fat	3
g fibre	3
g protein	12
g carbohydrate	25
mg cholesterol	18
mg sodium	417
mg potassium	294

Good: vitamin A, riboflavin, calcium, iron, niacin
Excellent: vitamin C

Easy Holiday Punch
In a punch bowl, combine
1 bottle (750 ml) each ginger ale
and cranberry juice and 1 small
container frozen orange juice
concentrate. Stir well and
add ice cubes before serving.

Citrus Sangria

White grape juice and citrus fruit make an elegant drink. Sparkling white grape juice is also nice to use instead of the grape juice and soda water.

1	lime	1
1	lemon	1
1	orange	1
1	bottle (1 litre) white grape juice	1
1	bottle (750 ml) soda water	1
	crushed ice cubes	

Cut lime, lemon and orange in half. Squeeze juice from one half of each; cut remaining halves into thin slices.

In large jug, combine grape juice, soda water, lime, lemon and orange slices and juice. Fill wine glasses one-quarter full with crushed ice. Pour in sangria and a slice of citrus. Makes 8 servings (8 fl oz/250 ml each).

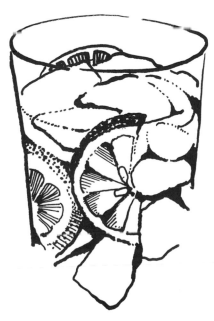

PER SERVING	
calories	85
g total fat	trace
g saturated fat	0
g fibre	trace
g protein	1
g carbohydrate	21
mg cholesterol	0
mg sodium	24
mg potassium	194

Gazpacho Cooler

Serve this at a brunch instead of Bloody Marys or as an alternative to an alcoholic drink. It tastes great and is packed with vitamin C.

¼	cucumber, peeled	¼
½	small onion	½
2	small tomatoes	2
¼	green pepper, seeded	¼
1	small garlic clove, crushed	1
16 fl oz	tomato juice	500 ml
2 tbsp	red wine vinegar or cider vinegar	30 ml
¼ tsp	dried dillweed	1.25 ml
Dash	hot pepper sauce	Dash
	pepper	
	lemon or lime slices	

Coarsely chop cucumber, onion, tomatoes and green pepper; transfer to blender. Add garlic and blend until smooth. Stir in tomato juice, vinegar, dillweed, hot pepper sauce, and pepper to taste.

Refrigerate for at least 1 hour or until chilled. Stir to mix well before pouring into glasses. Garnish with lemon or lime slice. Makes 6 servings (6 fl oz/175 ml each).

PER SERVING	
calories	27
g total fat	trace
g saturated fat	0
g fibre	1
g protein	1
g carbohydrate	6
mg cholesterol	0
mg sodium	297
mg potassium	300
Good: vitamin C	

Soups

A pea soup is one of the most nourishing soups you can make. Dried peas are an excellent source of soluble fibre (the kind that research has shown helps lower blood cholesterol) and potassium and a good source of iron and protein.

Old-Fashioned Pea Soup

Most recipes for this soup call for salt pork or a ham bone. In order to reduce fat, I don't use salt pork. I always make it when I have a ham bone, but you can make it without one. This soup is usually made with dried yellow soup peas, if they are not available, use yellow split peas. Try to use fresh savory, and not dried.

14 oz	dried yellow soup peas or split peas	400 g
4½ pts	water	2.5 lit
1	ham bone or 4 oz (125 g) ham, chopped	1
5	medium onions, chopped	5
3	medium carrots, peeled and chopped	3
2	celery sticks (including leaves), chopped	2
1 tsp	summer savory	5 ml
1	bay leaf	1
	salt and pepper	

Rinse peas. In a large pan, combine peas, water, ham bone or ham, onions, carrots, celery, summer savory and bay leaf; bring to boil. Skim off any scum. Cover and simmer for 3 hours or until peas are softened and soup has thickened. If soup is too thin, uncover and simmer 30 minutes longer. Season with salt and pepper to taste. Discard bay leaf and ham bone. Makes 8 servings, about ½ pt (300 ml) each.

PER SERVING	
calories	203
g total fat	2
g saturated fat	trace
g fibre	8
g protein	14
g carbohydrate	34
mg cholesterol	8
mg sodium	249
mg potassium	699
Good: niacin, iron	
Excellent: vitamin A, thiamin	

If you are on a low-salt diet, use water, homemade Chicken Stock (page 60) or a low-salt chicken or vegetable stock.

Summer Tomato and Green Bean Soup

Make this light soup in the summer when both green beans and tomatoes have the best flavour and fresh basil is readily available.

2 tsp	olive oil	10 ml
2	medium onions or leeks, chopped	2
3	medium carrots, chopped	3
1	large garlic clove, chopped	1
1 lb	green beans, cut in 1 in (2.5 cm) lengths	450 g
2½ pts	chicken stock	1.5 lit
1½ lb	tomatoes, diced	700 g
4 tbsp	chopped fresh basil or 1 tbsp (15 ml) dried	60 ml
	salt and pepper	

In a large pan, heat oil over medium heat; cook onions and carrots for 5 minutes. Add garlic, beans and stock; simmer for 20 minutes. Add tomatoes and simmer for 5 minutes. Add basil; season with salt and pepper to taste. Serve hot. Makes 8 servings, about 8 fl oz (250 ml) each.

PER SERVING	
calories	87
g total fat	2
g saturated fat	1
g fibre	3
g protein	6
g carbohydrate	12
mg cholesterol	0
mg sodium	616
mg potassium	554

Good: vitamin C, niacin
Excellent: vitamin A

If you are on a low-salt diet, use 3½ pts (2 lit) water instead of ¾ pts each stock and water. Sodium content per serving will then be 359 mg. If you omit the sausage as well, sodium content will be 54 mg per serving. Omitting the sausage will also reduce the fat content to 4 g per serving.

Smokey Sausage Lentil Soup

Lentils are an excellent source of fibre and are packed with nutrients – vegetable protein, iron, some calcium, and B-vitamins. If possible, make this main-course soup at the weekend or while you are cooking dinner one night to have a make-ahead dinner ready and waiting just to be reheated. We aren't supposed to have a lot of sausage because of its high fat content, so this is a good way to use a little for flavour.

1 tbsp	olive oil	15 ml
1	onion, chopped	1
4	celery sticks, sliced	4
6 oz	smoked sausage (such as kabanos), coarsely chopped	175 g
1¾ pts	chicken or vegetable stock	1 lit
1¾ pts	water	1 lit
1 lb	green lentils	450 g
1	strip (3 in/8 cm long) orange rind	1
1 tsp	crumbled dried marjoram	5 ml
1 tsp	crumbled dried savory	5 ml
3	carrots, peeled and sliced	3
2	potatoes, peeled and diced	2
	salt and pepper	

In a large heavy saucepan, heat oil over medium heat; add onion and cook for 5 minutes, stirring occasionally. Add celery and sausage; cook for 5 minutes, stirring occasionally.

Add stock, water, lentils, orange rind, marjoram and savory; bring to boil. Reduce heat, cover partially and simmer for 30 minutes.

Add carrots and potatoes; cover partially and simmer, stirring occasionally, for 35 minutes or until lentils are tender. Discard orange rind. Season with salt and pepper to taste. Makes 6 main-course servings, about ½ pt (300 ml) each.

PER SERVING	
calories	408
g total fat	12
g saturated fat	3
g fibre	9
g protein	25
g carbohydrate	52
mg cholesterol	19
mg sodium	871
mg potassium	1222

Good: riboflavin
Excellent: vitamin A, thiamin, niacin, iron

Dried Lentils

If using dried lentils, follow lentil soup recipe except substitute 6 oz (175 g) dried brown lentils for canned lentils and add 1¾ pts (1 lit) water with lentils. Cover and cook for 25 minutes or until lentils are tender, complete as in recipe.

Inexpensive lentils are a nutrient bargain—packed with all the good things we need such as protein, iron, the B vitamin niacin, complex carbohydrates and soluble fibre. They contain no cholesterol and very little fat. Dried lentils don't need to be soaked before cooking; red lentils cook in about 10 minutes, green in about 30 minutes.

Lentil Spinach Soup with Curried Yogurt

This soup is easy to make using either canned or dried lentils. (If using dried brown lentils, see information in margin.) The soup is packed with nutrients and along with toast and a salad makes a satisfying quick meal.

1¾ pts	chicken or vegetable stock	1 lit
1	can (15.2 oz/432 g) lentils, drained, or 1 lb (450 g) cooked lentils	1
2	celery sticks, chopped	2
2	small onions, finely chopped	2
2	small garlic cloves, crushed	2
10 oz	chopped fresh spinach	275 g
1 tbsp	lemon juice	15 ml
	salt and pepper	

Curried Yogurt

4 tbsp	low-fat yogurt	60 ml
1 tsp	curry powder	5 ml

In a saucepan, bring stock, lentils, celery, onions and garlic to boil; reduce heat, cover and simmer for 5 minutes. Add spinach and simmer for 3 minutes. Add lemon juice; season with salt and pepper to taste. (If thicker soup is desired, remove half and purée in food processor or blender; return to saucepan and heat through.)

Curried Yogurt: Mix yogurt with curry. Ladle soup into bowls; swirl dollop of curried yogurt into each. Makes 5 servings, about 8 fl oz (250 ml) each.

PER SERVING	
calories	136
g total fat	2
g saturated fat	trace
g fibre	4
g protein	12
g carbohydrate	19
mg cholesterol	1
mg sodium	825
mg potassium	773
Good: thiamin, riboflavin	
Excellent: vitamin A, niacin, iron	

To reduce salt and for a creamier soup, use 8 fl oz (250 ml) chicken stock and 1¼ pts (750 ml) milk.

Chunky Leek and Cabbage Soup

Because this is one of my favourite winter soups, I try to make enough to last for two nights. The first night, I enjoy the vegetables in pieces; the second night I purée the soup. If I don't have leeks to hand, I use 2 medium onions instead. If I have any fresh herbs – dill or thyme or basil – I add a tablespoon or two (15-30 ml) just before serving.

1	medium onion, chopped	1
1¼ pts	chicken stock	750 ml
6 oz	chopped leeks (white part mainly)	175 g
6 oz	peeled, diced potatoes	175 g
6 oz	chopped green cabbage	175 g
8 fl oz	milk	250 ml
	salt and pepper	
	chopped fresh dill, parsley or spring onions	

In a large saucepan, bring chicken stock, onion, leeks and potatoes to boil. Cover and reduce heat; simmer for about 20 minutes or until vegetables are tender.

Add cabbage; cook for 5 to 8 minutes or until tender. Stir in milk; season with salt and pepper to taste. Sprinkle each serving with dill, parsley or onions. Makes 6 servings, about 8 fl oz (250 ml) each.

PER SERVING	
calories	97
g total fat	2
g saturated fat	1
g fibre	2
g protein	5
g carbohydrate	16
mg cholesterol	3
mg sodium	420
mg potassium	406
Good: niacin	

Black Bean and Ham Soup

This is a great way to use up the end of a ham. Just leave a little meat on the bone and don't add any extra ham. Perfect for a casual supper along with toast and a green salad. I like to top each serving with sour cream or Greek-style yogurt and chopped tomato and spring onions.

14 oz	dried black (kidney) beans	400 g
2 tbsp	vegetable oil	30 ml
3	garlic cloves, crushed	3
4	onions, chopped	4
1	ham bone (optional)	1
8 oz	cooked ham, chopped	225 g
1	celery stick and leaves, chopped	1
1	bay leaf	1
1 tsp	each dried thyme, oregano and ground coriander	5 ml
3½ pts	water or beef stock	2 lit

Place beans in colander and wash. Transfer to a large pan and cover with 3½ pts (2 lit) water. Bring to boil; boil for 2 minutes. Remove from heat and cover; let stand for 1 hour, then drain.

In large heavy saucepan, heat oil over medium heat. Stir in garlic and onions; cook for 3 to 5 minutes or until softened.

Add beans, ham bone (if using), ham, celery, bay leaf, thyme, oregano and coriander. Pour in water or beef stock and bring to boil.

Reduce heat to medium-low; cover and simmer, stirring occasionally, for 1½ hours or until beans are tender. Discard bay leaf and bone.

Transfer about 1¾ pts (1 lit) to food processor or blender and purée; return to saucepan and stir to mix. Makes 10 servings, about 6 fl oz (175 ml) each.

PER SERVING (made with water)	
calories	189
g total fat	5
g saturated fat	1
g fibre	6
g protein	13
g carbohydrate	24
mg cholesterol	13
mg sodium	327
mg potassium	535

Good: niacin, iron
Excellent: thiamin

Quick and Easy Fish Chowder

If you keep a pack of fish fillets in your freezer, you can always make a meal at the last minute. Any fresh or frozen fillets can be used in this recipe. If I have bacon on hand, I'll use it for its smokey flavour. Sometimes I add chopped carrot or celery, and I always add fresh dill when I have it.

1 tbsp	olive oil or 4 slices bacon, chopped	15 ml
1	onion, chopped	1
3	potatoes*, diced	3
16 fl oz	water	500 ml
1 lb	fresh or frozen fish fillets, cut in chunks	450 g
16 fl oz	milk	500 ml
8 oz	sweetcorn kernels (frozen or canned)	225 g
4 tbsp	coarsely chopped fresh parsley or dill	60 ml
	salt and pepper	

In a heavy saucepan, heat oil over medium heat (or cook bacon and drain off fat). Add onion and cook for 5 minutes or until tender. Add potatoes and water; cover and simmer until vegetables are nearly tender, about 15 minutes.

Add fish; cover and cook until opaque, about 2 minutes for fresh, 10 minutes for frozen.

Stir in milk and sweetcorn; simmer until hot. Add parsley or dill. Season with salt and pepper to taste. Makes 4 main-course servings, about 13 fl oz (375 ml) each.

---

* I only peel potatoes if the skin is tough. Unpeeled potatoes have nearly twice as much fibre.

PER SERVING	(without bacon)
calories	301
g total fat	6
g saturated fat	2
g fibre	3
g protein	27
g carbohydrate	36
mg cholesterol	66
mg sodium	179
mg potassium	1065
Good: thiamin, riboflavin, calcium	
Excellent: niacin	

When using canned salmon, be sure to crush bones and include in soup. The bones are an excellent source of calcium.

Hearty Salmon Chowder

I first had this delicious soup when it was served to a group of food writers on a boat off British Columbia's Vancouver Island. We all asked for the recipe, which was from the *Lopez Island Cookbook*. Here it is adapted slightly. You could also use semi-skimmed milk instead of evaporated milk; however, I like the flavour with evaporated milk. It is a good recipe to remember when planning a camping or boat trip.

1	can (6.5 oz/185 g) salmon	1
2 tsp	olive oil	10 ml
2 oz	each chopped onion and celery	50 g
2 oz	chopped green pepper	50 g
1	garlic clove, chopped	1
3	medium potatoes, diced	3
2	medium carrots, diced	2
8 fl oz	each chicken stock and water	250 ml
½ tsp	each coarse pepper and dill seed	2.5 ml
8 oz	courgettes, diced	225 g
1	can (14 oz/400 g) evaporated milk	1
1	can (10 oz/280 g) cream-style corn	1
	pepper	
1 oz	chopped fresh parsley (optional)	25 g

Drain and flake salmon, reserving liquid

In a large non-stick saucepan, heat oil over medium heat; cook onion, celery, green pepper and garlic, stirring often, for 5 minutes or until vegetables are tender.

Add potatoes, carrots, chicken stock, water, pepper and dill seed; bring to boil. Reduce heat, cover and simmer for 20 minutes or until vegetables are tender. Add courgettes; simmer, covered, for 5 minutes.

Add salmon, reserved liquid, evaporated milk, corn, and pepper to taste. Cook over low heat just until heated through. Just before serving, add parsley. Makes 4 main-course servings (14 fl oz/ 425 ml each) or 8 appetizer servings (6 fl oz/175 ml each).

PER MAIN-COURSE SERVING	
calories	359
g total fat	8
g saturated fat	3
g fibre	5
g protein	20
g carbohydrate	54
mg cholesterol	20
mg sodium	758
mg potassium	1194

Good: thiamin
Excellent: vitamins A and C, riboflavin, niacin, calcium

Creamy Clam Chowder

This is a favourite of mine for an easy supper, but it also makes a wonderful appetizer course on its own. You can use canned oysters instead of clams.

1 tbsp	vegetable oil	15 ml
1	small onion, diced	1
1	celery stick, diced	1
1	carrot, diced	1
2 tbsp	plain flour	30 ml
4 fl oz	fish stock or white wine	125 ml
1	can (5 oz/142 g) clams or oysters	1
1	potato, peeled and diced	1
1 tsp	dried thyme or 1 tbsp (15 ml) fresh	5 ml
1 pt	milk	600 ml
2 tbsp	chopped fresh parsley	30 ml
	salt and pepper	

In a large saucepan, heat oil over medium heat; cook onion, celery and carrot, covered, for 5 minutes. Blend in flour. Stirring constantly, gradually pour in stock or white wine. Drain liquid from clams into pan; set clams aside. Add potatoes and thyme; stir and bring to boil. Reduce heat and simmer, uncovered, until potatoes are tender, about 10 minutes.

Add clams, milk and parsley; cook just until heated through. Season with salt and pepper to taste. Makes 3 main-course servings of 11 fl oz (325 ml) each or 6 appetizer servings of 5 fl oz (150 ml) each.

PER MAIN-COURSE SERVING	
calories	255
g total fat	8
g saturated fat	3
g fibre	2
g protein	12
g carbohydrate	30
mg cholesterol	35
mg sodium	333
mg potassium	655

Good: vitamin C, niacin
Excellent: vitamin A, riboflavin, calcium, iron

Beef 'n' Bean Minestrone

Packed with nutrients, this easy main-course soup is great to have on hand for those nights when everyone is busy. The soup keeps well in the refrigerator for up to three days, ready and waiting for anyone to warm up a bowlful in the microwave. This version is lighter than many recipes because the vegetables aren't sautéed in oil.

8 oz	lean minced beef	225 g
1	large onion, diced	1
1	carrot, diced	1
1	celery stick, diced	1
1	small courgette (6 in/15 cm) diced	1
2	tomatoes or 1 can (14 oz/397 g) undrained, chopped	2
1	potato, peeled and diced	1
3	garlic cloves, chopped	3
3½ pts	water	2 lit
3 oz	small pasta	75 g
1 tsp	each dried oregano and basil or 2 tbsp (30 ml) each fresh*	5 ml
1	can (15.2 oz/432 g) white cannellini beans, drained	1
1 oz	freshly grated Parmesan cheese	25 g
1 oz	chopped fresh parsley	25 g
	salt and pepper	

In a large saucepan, cook meat over medium heat until brown, breaking up with fork; drain off fat. Add onion; cook, stirring, for 3 minutes.

Add carrot, celery, courgettes, tomatoes, potato and garlic; cook, stirring, for 3 minutes. Add water; bring to boil.

Add pasta, oregano and basil; cook, uncovered, until pasta is tender but firm and vegetables are cooked, 10 to 12 minutes.

Add cannellini beans, Parmesan and parsley; season with salt and pepper to taste. Makes 8 servings, about ½ pt (300 ml) each.

PER SERVING

calories	203
g total fat	4
g saturated fat	2
g fibre	7
g protein	13
g carbohydrate	29
mg cholesterol	16
mg sodium	337
mg potassium	589

Good: niacin, iron
Excellent: vitamin A

* If using fresh herbs add just before serving.

Puree of Carrot and Parsnip

Parsnips add a sweet flavour to this easy-to-make soup. It can be prepared in advance and refrigerated up to 3 days or frozen for up to 2 months. If you make it ahead of time, add the milk just before serving.

1 tsp	vegetable oil	5 ml
4	medium carrots, chopped	4
2	medium parsnips, peeled and chopped	2
1	small onion, chopped	1
1	medium potato, peeled and chopped	1
1¼ pts	vegetable or chicken stock	750 ml
12 fl oz	milk	375 ml
	chives or chopped spring onion	

In a large saucepan or microwaveable dish, toss oil with carrots, parsnips, onion and potato; cover and cook over low heat for 20 minutes or microwave at high (100%) power for 10 minutes or until vegetables are tender.

Stir in stock; bring to boil. Reduce heat and simmer, covered, for 30 minutes or microwave, covered, at high (100%) power for 15 minutes.

In a food processor or blender, process mixture in batches until smooth; return soup to pan. Stir in milk; reheat without boiling.

When serving, sprinkle each bowlful with chives or chopped spring onion. Makes 8 servings, about 6 fl oz (175 ml) each.

PER SERVING	
calories	95
g total fat	2
g saturated fat	1
g fibre	2
g protein	4
g carbohydrate	15
mg cholesterol	3
mg sodium	336
mg potassium	385
Excellent: vitamin A	

Most stocks made from a cube are high in salt. If you are on a low-salt diet, you might want to make your own stock.

Easiest Chicken Stock

Pour all the pan drippings from a roast chicken into a jar; cover and refrigerate. Discard fat from top. Use remaining gelatinous mixture to flavour soups or dilute with water for stock.

Stock from a Cube

Because these are high in salt, use double the amount of water that is called for on the packet.

Curried Pumpkin Soup

This wonderful autumn soup is a recipe from my friends and good cooks Peter and Penny White. It has only a hint of curry flavour so as not to mask the pumpkin, and is best made ahead so that the flavours develop.

1 tbsp	vegetable oil	15 ml
2 oz	finely chopped onion	50 g
1	garlic clove, chopped	1
8 oz	fresh mushrooms, sliced	225 g
2 tbsp	plain flour	30 ml
1 tsp	curry powder	5 ml
16 fl oz	Chicken Stock (page 60)	500 ml
1 lb	fresh pumpkin, peeled and cooked	450 g
1 tbsp	runny honey	15 ml
	freshly grated nutmeg	
16 fl oz	milk	500 ml

   In a large saucepan, heat oil over medium heat; cook onion, garlic and mushrooms for 8 to 10 minutes or until softened. Stir in flour and curry powder; cook for 1 minute over low heat, stirring, until well blended.

   Gradually add stock, whisking until smooth. Stir in pumpkin and honey; season with nutmeg to taste. Cook over low heat for 15 minutes, stirring occasionally. (Soup can be prepared to this point, covered and refrigerated for up to 2 days.)

   Add milk and heat until hot. Makes 8 servings, about 6 fl oz (175 ml) each.

PER SERVING	
calories	94
g total fat	3
g saturated fat	1
g fibre	1
g protein	5
g carbohydrate	13
mg cholesterol	5
mg sodium	241
mg potassium	342
Excellent: vitamin A	

If possible, make this soup a day in advance, cover and refrigerate. Any fat from the soup bone will harden on top and can be easily removed.

Barley is high in soluble fibre, which is the kind of fibre that research has shown lowers blood cholesterol.

Old-Fashioned Mushroom Barley Soup

Barley makes an excellent base for soups: it's inexpensive, filling and nutritious. Many butchers are delighted to cut up soup bones and give them away. This is a basic recipe: add other vegetables such as leeks, green beans, cabbage, turnip, sweet potato or pumpkin.

3½ pts	water	2 lit
3 oz	pot or pearl barley	75 g
1	large soup bone (beef or lamb)	1
1	bay leaf	1
3	large carrots, chopped	3
1	celery stick (including leaves), chopped	1
1	large onion, chopped	1
1	large potato, peeled and diced	1
1	garlic clove, chopped	1
¼ tsp	dried thyme	1.25 ml
4 oz	coarsely chopped mushrooms	125 g
	salt and pepper	

In a large pan, combine water, barley, soup bone and bay leaf; bring to boil. Reduce heat, cover and simmer for 1 hour.

Add carrots, celery, onion, potato, garlic and thyme; simmer, covered, for 25 minutes. Add mushrooms and simmer for 5 minutes or until tender. Season with salt and pepper to taste. Remove bay leaf and soup bone. Makes 8 hearty servings, ½ pt (300 ml) each.

PER SERVING	
calories	83
g total fat	trace
g saturated fat	0
g fibre	3
g protein	2
g carbohydrate	19
mg cholesterol	0
mg sodium	30
mg potassium	243
Excellent: vitamin A	

Right:
Chinese Noodle and Mushroom Soup (page 58), Quick Bean, Broccoli and Tomato Chowder (page 59), Creamy Clam Chowder (page 52)